What *Really* Happens after We Die

James L. Papandrea

What *Really* Happens after We Die

There *Will* Be Hugs in Heaven

SOPHIA INSTITUTE PRESS
Manchester, New Hampshire

Sophia Institute Press
Box 5284, Manchester, NH 03108
1-800-888-9344

www.SophiaInstitute.com

Sophia Institute Press® is a registered trademark of Sophia Institute.

Library of Congress Cataloging-in-Publication Data

Names: Papandrea, James L., 1963- author.
Title: What really happens after we die: there will be hugs in heaven /
  James L. Papandrea.
Description: Manchester, New Hampshire : Sophia Institute Press, 2019.
  Includes bibliographical references. Summary: "Dr. James Papandrea
  gathers here in one place all that is known about the afterlife—drawn
  from the teachings of Jesus, the Apostles, the Church Fathers, and the
  Church's Magisterium—affording a complete, authoritative, detailed
  portrait of the state of souls after death"— Provided by publisher.
Identifiers: LCCN 2019037483 ISBN 9781622826384 (paperback) ISBN
  9781622826391 (epub)
Subjects: LCSH: Future life—Catholic Church.
Classification: LCC BT903 .P37 2019 DDC 236/.2—dc23
LC record available at https://lccn.loc.gov/2019037483

Third printing

For Frank Papandrea (1937–2018),
"Uncle Frank"

Emmaus

Under my feet a dusty road, over my shoulder a heavy load,
Miles to go before I'm done, and I'm losing a race with the
setting sun.
My eyes so full of tears I couldn't see
Who it was that was walking next to me.
   He walked on the water, He turned water into wine.
   He calmed an angry storm on the sea.
   He called a man out of the grave and gave him back his life.
   Can He calm the storm inside of me?
   Can He calm the storm inside of me?
I need a rest from the weary road, need to put down my heavy load.
My heart on fire all the way, so I begged Him to stay,
And in the breaking of the bread my eyes were clear.
My Savior, my Christ is here.
   He walked on the water, He turned water into wine.
   He calmed an angry storm on the sea.
   He called the blind out of their blindness and gave them
back their sight
   And He opened up my eyes and set me free
   And He calmed the angry storm inside of me.
   He opened up my eyes and set me free.
He walked on water, and He walks with me.

From the album *Still Quiet Voice*, by Jim L. Papandrea

Contents

What *Really* Happens after We Die

1

It's a Wonderful Afterlife

Johnny laughed to himself—or rather, at himself—as he pulled on his flannel jacket. Being the boss was supposed to have perks. It was supposed to mean less time out on the road, less time in the truck. It was supposed to mean less work, not more. And wasn't there some vague expectation of the owner of the business getting to wear fancier clothes? He set his lunchbox on the passenger seat and started up the truck. He paused for a moment more, listening to the echo of the diesel engine in the driveway. He reminded himself to be thankful, and then he put it in reverse, and backed into his day.

As the truck pulled into the strip-mall parking lot, a larger-than-usual group of men was milling around in front of the big-box builder's store. They all moved in the direction of Johnny and his truck. They moved somewhat humbly, heads a little down, but purposefully. He knew that walk. He had seen his father walk that same way, many years ago, before he was known as Johnny, when everyone called him Juan. He was only one generation away from that walk.

As few words as possible were exchanged—all in Spanish —about the project for the day. "*Cinco,*" Johnny said, as he held up five fingers. Five men climbed into the back of his truck, and without looking at the others still standing there, he pulled out of the parking lot.

Lunchtime came, and the project was behind schedule. Annoyed, Johnny had to make a trip to the store for some last-minute supplies. When he got there, he saw that there were still some men standing by the front door, bouncing on the balls of their feet to keep themselves warm. Coming out of the store, the men looked at Johnny, and he couldn't look away. He nodded and then walked to his truck. But as he backed out of his parking spot, he stopped. *What the heck*, he thought. He spun the truck around and drove up in front of the door. "*Tres.*" Three men got into the truck bed. Johnny sighed. "*Cinco—dos mas.*" And two more men jumped into the back.

Three o'clock came, and the project was back on schedule. Time for a coffee break. Johnny got his coffee to go, but from the drive-through, he could see that there was still a small group of men in front of the store, hoping for work. These were the guys who hadn't given up at one o'clock or two. These were the guys who really didn't want to go home and tell their families there was no work that day. With five more men in the back of his truck, Johnny arrived at the site with less than two hours left in the day. But it didn't matter. There were too many workers now, and the project was finished after the last group of men had worked for only half an hour. Johnny gave them some busy work and had everyone clean up the site, and when five o'clock finally rolled around, he gathered the men and pulled out his wallet.

Johnny knew exactly which guys had worked all day, and they did too. The first group of five lined up first. Johnny handed each one of them a new hundred dollar bill. The next group of men—the ones who started after lunch—now lined up, hoping to get half that much. Johnny gave each one of them a new hundred dollar bill. He did the same with the last group of five. One hundred dollars for less than two hours of work. Johnny couldn't look any of the men in the eye. He didn't want to have to try to explain. Just paying it forward.

A couple of men from the first group grumbled that it was not fair. Johnny just shook his head and said, "Well ... I'm the boss."

Every Time a Bell Rings . . .

As you were reading that story about Johnny and his workers, you probably figured out somewhere along the way that it was a version of Jesus' parable of the laborers (Matt. 20:1–16). This is one of several parables that Jesus begins by saying, "The Kingdom of Heaven is like this ..." These are stories that Jesus used to teach about God's priorities and the way God does things, and about what Heaven is like, because after all, Heaven is where God's will is done the way it should be done on earth. The story is an analogy—that is, the elements of the story represent more important things. In this case, the landowner represents God, and the laborers represent, well ... us—people whose lives are dedicated to God in some way. And one meaning that we can get from this parable (because parables often have multiple meanings) is that it doesn't matter that some of us seem to do more for God in our lives than others, or that some of us come to know Jesus later in life. When the work is over, we all get the same reward. Not because we've earned it. Not because it's fair. But because we all get more than we deserve. But what is that reward? It's obviously not money. So what does the money represent in the parable? If "the Kingdom of Heaven is like this," then the reward must be Heaven itself. But what does that mean?

What *Really* Happens after We Die

Whatever it is, it has to do with what Jesus called *resurrection*. Sure, looking back on it now, we all think we know what resurrection is, but back then — especially before Jesus' own Resurrection — there was a lot of confusion about it. Well, that's what this book is about. For now, we'll just note that Jesus said we will be "sons of the resurrection." I'm tempted to translate that as "children of the resurrection" or "sons and daughters of the resurrection," and that would not be wrong, but the point of being "sons" in the world of Jesus and the apostles is that sons are heirs. When Jesus says that we (even the women) are "sons" of the resurrection, He is saying that we are *heirs* of the resurrection. It is our inheritance. It is the reward.

I remember as a kid being particularly affected by a movie called *The Littlest Angel* (1969), starring a young Johnny Whitaker as a shepherd boy who dies and finds himself in Heaven — as an angel. Although I was a little disturbed by seeing the depiction of a kid about my age dying in an accident, Whitaker's character isn't really phased by that. His biggest problem is that his angel robe has no pockets. Or maybe you're more familiar with the movie that everyone watches around Christmastime, *It's a Wonderful Life* (1946). This film deserves all the attention it has received over the years, but it, too, has an element that is based on the assumption that when people die, they become angels. Clarence the angel used to be a regular human, and now on his first assignment as a guardian angel, he has to talk George Bailey out of committing suicide. In the process, George learns that every time you hear a bell ring, an angel is graduating from flight school.

Do we become angels when we die? Most Christians today probably know that we do not become angels. The angels in the Bible are an entirely separate thing — spiritual beings created by

God who come from the spiritual realm, but who are sometimes used as messengers in our world. In fact, that's why they are called "angels": the Greek word *angelos* means "messenger." But Jesus did say that in the Kingdom, we would be *like* angels (Matt. 22:30; Mark 12:25; Luke 20:36). What did he mean by that? He seems to mean that our *life* in Heaven will be the life of an angel—that our vocation will be to worship and serve God, as opposed to a vocation such as marriage. In fact, Jesus tells us that there will be no marriage in the afterlife. But we'll get to that later.

Apparently in the early centuries of the Church, they had their versions of *The Littlest Angel* and *It's a Wonderful Life*, because people were asking the question "Do we become angels?" Some of the Church Fathers felt compelled to answer the question. No, they said, we do not become angels. St. Jerome, in letters to a couple of laypeople named Theodora (Letter 75) and Eustochium (Letter 108), wrote that to become angels would be to cease to be human, and the afterlife is not the end of our humanity. We do not cease to be human, he said. "The apostle Paul will still be Paul." In fact, as we will see, in the afterlife our humanity is not relinquished; it is perfected.

Ashes to Ashes and Dust to Dust

We used to use the expression "man on the street" for a reporter who stood outside somewhere with a microphone, asking questions of random people walking by. It was supposed to be like taking an opinion poll of regular folks. Now, of course, reporters can be women, too, so we don't use this expression anymore. But I suspect that if you took a "person on the street" poll of people who profess to be Christian, and you asked them what happens when a person dies, most would say something like, "Your soul leaves your body, and it goes to Heaven." Their assumption would be that the body is left to decay in the ground, and the human soul or spirit goes on to a life lived in the spiritual realm. And that's not entirely wrong—but it is incomplete. And if anyone thinks that this is the end of the story, then that's a real problem, because Jesus, the apostles, and the Church Fathers all taught that this was not the end of the story.

In fact, it was the pagans (philosophers) and heretics (gnostics) who said that the afterlife would be a purely spiritual—that is, disembodied—existence. They believed that the things of the material world were inferior to the things of the spiritual realm, and some of them went so far as to say that the things of the physical world were inherently evil, while only the things of the spiritual realm could be good (for more on this, see the sections on docetism and gnosticism in my books *Reading the Early Church Fathers* and *The Earliest Christologies*). But this teaching of the philosophers and gnostics directly contradicted the Judeo-Christian conviction that creation is good. Creation is good because the Creator is good. Still, the philosophers and the gnostics maintained that the human body was something vile, a prison to be escaped at the time of death, a shell to be discarded, as a snake sheds its skin. And for this reason, they rejected and denied the Christian doctrine of the resurrection.

The Church Fathers tell us that we do not become angels, because angels are purely spiritual and live a purely spiritual existence. But as we will see, our existence in the afterlife will not be purely spiritual—it will be in some sense corporeal; that is, as humans we are embodied beings, and we will again be embodied in the resurrection. So whatever "resurrection" means, it cannot mean being raised to an existence that is spiritual only—if we believed that, then we would be no different from the philosophers and the gnostics. No, when Jesus talked about resurrection (not to mention when He was raised Himself), He was teaching us something else. The word He used for "resurrection" (or the Greek word that the authors of the Gospels used to translate His Aramaic word) was *anastasis*. It means to stand again, to return to an upright position. That's not a word that means to go from bodily to spiritual, or from tangible to ethereal. It means to return to the "stasis," or position, we once held. My students often ask me why we say that Jesus "rose *again*." Was He resurrected more than once? It's a fair question, because the expression is kind of a confusing idiom in English. But the point is that He was standing once, then He died, and then He was standing again. In His Resurrection, He "stood again." And so will we.

Ashes to ashes and dust to dust is not the end of the story. It's true that our bodies will decay for a time, but they will also be restored in the resurrection and reunited with our spirits to make us once again the complete human beings we were created to be.

So, what happens when we die? What do we mean when we say our souls leave our bodies? Are our bodies disposable shells, or are they an essential part of who we are as humans? Do we retain our personalities, or are our souls just absorbed into the universe? What is the Kingdom of Heaven? This book will attempt to answer all of these questions, as much as possible. We will make this attempt with the help of Jesus, His apostles, and the Church Fathers (and Mothers) who received the teachings of the apostles and passed them on to us. We'll say as much as we can, and then we'll accept that at the end of the day, there is much about this that's still a mystery. How could it be otherwise? Heaven has to be something that you can't really understand until you get there. So, we have to admit at the beginning that we can know only a limited amount about this, as though we are looking through a dark glass (see 1 Cor. 13:9–13). And yet it's exactly this kind of present limitation that will be lifted in the resurrection. When that time comes, it will not be more dim, smoky glass and mirrors, as the pagans thought. It will be glory and clarity.

2

It's Not What You Think

There it is . . . the corner office. Dave smirked as he looked up at the window far above the chaos of Wall Street. He had made it: executive position in one of the largest brokerage firms in the world. As he walked on, he congratulated himself for his determined rise up the corporate and social ladders. And the best part was that he was finally in a position to hire other people to do all the annoying little tasks that used to drive him nuts. No more laundry. No more cleaning the apartment. No more grocery shopping. No more putting gas in the car. No more trips to the dry cleaners or the post office. No time for that stuff.

Dave was startled out of his daydream by Larry, one of the more aggressive of the homeless men who hung around the area. Larry stepped right into Dave's path, forcing him to stop walking. With eyes down at the ground, Larry went into his usual story about needing a little help, if the gentleman could spare some change. Dave looked around. *Where are the cops when you need them? Why can't they get rid of these people?* Dave shook his head without saying a word and walked around Larry, waving a hand to dismiss him, just as he did every day. He wished he could pay someone else to be annoyed by the homeless for him. And get his teeth cleaned for him. And get that colonoscopy for him . . .

What *Really* Happens after We Die

When the elevator opened at the top of one of the largest brokerage firms in the world, its newest executive was lying on the floor, dead. Larry also died that night. It might have been exposure, it might have been alcoholism, but no one bothered to do an autopsy. Sure, Larry was a drunk, but he had seen some stuff that you can't unsee. And even in his darkest times, he never stopped believing in the promises of God. So God kept His promises and welcomed Larry into Paradise.

Dave was another story. He knew about God but thought he was too smart, too evolved, for religion. So he chose not to have a relationship with God. And when the time came, God honored that choice and let Dave go to Hell. In Hell Dave was tortured by his own regret. He was also tormented by the knowledge that Larry was in Heaven. Stuck in the bargaining stage of his self-pity, Dave thought to himself, *Well, it might be too little, too late, but it couldn't hurt to pray.* Of course, there was no way he was going to pray to God—he still had some pride, after all! So, he prayed to the only person he knew who he could be certain was in Heaven. He prayed to Larry. *Larry, if you can hear me, can you put in a good word for me with the Big Guy and see about getting me outa here?*

To his surprise, Dave got an answer to his prayer. In his torment, he could hear the voice of Larry. *Dave, I prayed for you every day you walked past me. And I would pray for you now, except that I've already received the answer to my prayers. You were offered forgiveness many times in your life, but you refused it. To reject forgiveness is the unforgiveable sin. It's too late for you. You can't get here from there.*

Dave's heart sank, but in his despair, he had a moment of selflessness. *Okay, I get that. But the other guys in my firm. Pray for them.*

Larry sighed. *Sorry, Dave. They might have had a chance to turn themselves around if they could have heard the Gospel read at your funeral. But they all got together and decided that you should be honored with a nonreligious memorial.*

We Ain't Afraid of No Ghosts

If the afterlife is not what most people assume it is, then we should take a step back and see what Jesus Himself and the apostles, who were His closest disciples, taught about it. The story of Dave and Larry is, of course, an adaptation of the parable of the rich man and Lazarus (Luke 16:19–31). In this famous story, we see two men, a rich man and a hopelessly poor man. What you have to keep in mind is that many people in the ancient world would have assumed that any rich person was rich precisely because he or she was blessed by God—and that meant that the person was holy. And people would also assume that the poor man was poor because he was being punished by God. So, the idea that the rich guy goes to Hell and the poor guy goes to Heaven—right at the start, that turns a lot of people's assumptions upside down. That's one of the reasons Jesus told this parable—to make the point that you can't assume a person's holiness by his or her prosperity.

But in addition to this major point, the parable brings up a lot of interesting questions about the afterlife. What does it mean to be tormented in the afterlife? To what extent can we communicate with (pray to) the dead, without falling into the occult practice of necromancy (Deut. 18:9–14)? And does the "chasm" between Hell and Heaven mean that there is no hope for conversion after physical death? Remember that this is a parable, so when Jesus tells this story, He is not implying that it's a true story—only that it is an illustration to make His point. So, we have to be careful not to take literally every detail of a parable. Still, these are important questions, and the parable does seem to hint at some answers. We will return to these questions in the course of this book.

But if we have established that we do not become angels when we die, do we become ghosts? We are all familiar with ghost stories that assume that the ghosts are the souls of the dead, perhaps lost, perhaps lingering over some unfinished business, maybe even haunting the living out of anger or a desire for revenge. Many Christians today would assume that anything thought to be appearances of ghosts is demonic activity, meant to distract people from God with an obsession for the occult, or simply scare them out of their trust in God. This is certainly possible, and the demonic should not be ruled out. But the Church Fathers also believed that it was possible for the souls of the dead to remain in our realm awhile before moving on to the next life.

The Eastern bishop Gregory of Nyssa (bishop from 372 to 395) wrote a treatise called *On the Soul and Resurrection*, which is very important for our study of the afterlife. In that document, Gregory records a conversation with his older sister and teacher, Macrina. The conversation may very well be idealized and embellished with Gregory's own thoughts put into the words of his sister, but we know that she was, in fact, his first catechist, and that she was an influential early Church leader in her own right. In any case, the teachings in the document were obviously approved by Gregory and accepted by the Church Fathers.

In the course of the conversation, Macrina accepts the possibility of ghosts, "shadowy phantoms of the departed," seen "around their graves." She says they are likely the souls of those who are still attached to this life. In other words, the person's soul refuses to leave the earth at the time of death because that person was too attached to earthly life and not focused enough on the things of Heaven (see Matt. 6:19–21). So, the soul lingers near the remains of the body, and "hovers regretfully over the place where its material is, and continues to haunt it."

The idea that the soul of a dead person can hang around after death can be found in pre-Christian philosophers, especially in Plato's treatise *On the Soul* (*Phaedo*). But while the early Church Fathers had no problem rejecting other aspects of Plato's thought on the subject, they seemed to accept the possibility of ghosts. For our purposes, the point is that it is not the case that all souls become ghosts. If any do, it is only those souls who are not going on to Heaven, since they are clearly too attached to the present life to have had any kind of relationship with God. So, I would venture to say that it's safe to assume that if you are reading this book, you will not become a ghost.

I should also point out that it's possible to have a vision of someone who has died, and that does not mean that the person is a ghost. If you believe that you have had a vision of a loved one who has passed on, that vision may be a gift from God, meant to give you comfort. There are many times throughout the history of the Church when people have reported dreams or visions of their loved ones who have joined the saints in the next life. This does not mean that these people are ghosts and certainly does not imply that they are lingering on the earthly plane before moving on. Not all apparitions are ghosts, and that's about as much as I think I can say on the subject.

But there's still an important point to notice here. Ghost stories are meant to scare us, and there's a reason for that. Why are ghosts scary? Because they are damned. There is no hope for them, and therefore there is a desperate despair about them that reminds us of our own mortality and the seriousness of making sure that we don't end up like that. After all, isn't this the message of the ghost of Jacob Marley in Charles Dickens's classic *A*

Christmas Carol? And it's also the message of Jesus' parable of the rich man and Lazarus. Don't end up like Dave. It's a cautionary tale.

On one level, we are supposed to take our mortality seriously, because Jesus clearly implied on several occasions that once we die, there is no going back and undoing the choices we made in this life. The parable of the rich man and Lazarus certainly implies that this is the case, and so do the parables of the ten bridesmaids, the unmerciful servant, and the wedding banquet. But on another level, we Christians should not fear death, because God has promised that, for us, it is a doorway to eternal life.

St. Ambrose, bishop of Milan (bishop from 374 to 397), wrote this in a treatise called *On Belief in the Resurrection*:

> It is said, indeed, that there have been certain tribes who mourned at the birth of human beings, and kept festival at their deaths, and this not without reason, for they thought that those who had entered upon this ocean of life should be mourned over, but that they who had escaped from the waves and storms of this world should be accompanied by rejoicing, not without good reason. And we too forget the birthdays of the departed, and commemorate with festal solemnity the day on which they died.... Death is not an evil, because it is the refuge from all miseries and all evils, a safe harbor of security, and a haven of rest.... So then, death is not only not an evil, but is even a good thing ... and if one consider accurately, it [death] is not the death of our being, but of evil, for being continues; it is evil that perishes.

When Jesus talked about death, He used the metaphor of a grain of wheat. He said, "Truly, truly, I say to you, unless a grain of wheat falls into the earth and dies, it remains alone; but if it dies, it bears much fruit. He who loves his life loses it, and he who hates his life in this world will keep it for eternal life" (John 12:24–25). In other words, you can't get to eternity in the next life unless you are willing to let go of this one. You can't get to Heaven unless you die. But the good news is that death is not the end, and those who die in Christ do not die alone but, in reality, pass through the door of death into a new, eternal life. But what does that life look like?

Jesus also said, "I have come down from heaven, not to do my own will, but the will of him who sent me; and this is the will of him who sent me, that I should lose nothing of all that he has given me, but raise it up at the last day. For this is the will of my Father, that every one who sees the Son and believes in him should have eternal life; and I will raise him up at the last day" (John 6:38–40). Eternal life is to be "raised up." Here Jesus is referring to the resurrection "at the last day."

When St. Paul had to write to the Thessalonian Christians about the deaths of their loved ones, he said that although we do grieve our loss, we do not grieve the same way "as others do who have no hope" (1 Thess. 4:13). Ours is a hopeful grief, because, although we are sad for ourselves, having lost our loved ones for a time, we are not sad for our loved ones. Sometimes we forget that this is a very important difference between Christian grief and the grief of unbelievers. We mourn because we will miss our loved ones — not because they are lost or have ceased to exist. We entrust them to the care of God and His mercy, and we know that they have come to rest in that safe harbor that St. Ambrose wrote about.

But Paul did have to make sure his Thessalonian audience understood what it meant to die in Christ. He went on:

For since we believe that Jesus died and rose again, even so, through Jesus, God will bring with him those who have fallen asleep. For this we declare to you by the word of the Lord, that we who are alive, who are left until the coming of the Lord, shall not precede those who have fallen asleep. For the Lord himself will descend from heaven with a cry of command, with the archangel's call, and with the sound of the trumpet of God. And the dead in Christ will rise first; then we who are alive, who are left, shall be caught up together with them in the clouds to meet the Lord in the air; and so we shall always be with the Lord. Therefore comfort one another with these words. (1 Thess. 4:14–18)

What Paul is saying here is that the Thessalonians did not have to worry that their loved ones who had passed away might miss out on the return of Jesus. They would not be late for the second coming—in fact, they had gone on ahead. And when Jesus returns, they will be there with Him, and anyone who happens to be alive at the time of the second coming will also be "caught up" with them. This is highly symbolic language—Paul is using the kind of apocalyptic metaphors that we find in the Old Testament prophets and in the book of Revelation. In fact, the idea of being "caught up" into the clouds reminds us of when Enoch (Gen. 5:24) and Elijah (2 Kings 2:11) were taken up into Heaven.

But don't get sidetracked by interpretations that talk of a "rapture." Although it's true that the word "rapture" comes from the Latin word for "caught up," there is no indication here of a two-step second coming, in which Jesus comes back temporarily to take some people away and then comes back later for the

glorified, empowered, spiritual, and immortal: the original good-ness of the body, without the sins of the flesh.

So, a spiritual body is a body that is suited to the spiritual realm. It is incorruptible — that is, it does not decay. It is restored to the purity of God's original creation. And it is immortal. Some of the Church Fathers would add that the resurrection body is impassible — that is, it is incapable of suffering (see, for example, Tertullian, *On the Resurrection of the Flesh* 57 and Rev. 21:4).

Jesus Is the Prototype

St. Paul begins his teaching on the resurrection body this way: "But someone will ask, 'How are the dead raised? With what kind of body do they come?' You foolish man! What you sow does not come to life unless it dies" (1 Cor. 15:35–36). Ever the diplomat, Paul first calls the questioner a fool and then refers him back to Jesus and the metaphor of the grain of wheat. But notice that when Jesus used that metaphor, He was talking as much about His own Death and Resurrection as about the general resurrection of believers. In other words, if we want to know more about the resurrection and the spiritual body, we can look at Jesus' resurrection body, and that will give us some clues about our own.

Writing about the Incarnation, the apostle John said, "The Word became flesh and dwelt among us, full of grace and truth; we have beheld his glory, glory as of the only Son from the Father" (John 1:14). When did the apostles behold the glory of Jesus? Certainly we could say that whenever Jesus healed the sick or fed the crowds, His glory was breaking through into the world. But in general, Jesus' human life was a veiling of His glory, as He humbled Himself to take on true humanity (see Phil. 2:6–11). However, the apostles saw His glory in a very direct way on two occasions. One was the Transfiguration, and the other, of course, was His Resurrection.

We read in the Gospels that, on one occasion, Jesus took Peter, James, and John up to a mountainous place to pray. While they were there, they saw a momentary revelation of Jesus' glory (see Matt. 17:1–8; Mark 9:2–10; Luke 9:28–36; 1 Pet. 1:16–18). He appeared to them to be emanating light, His face shining like the sun, and His garments as bright as light. They saw Him talking with Elijah and Moses, indicating that they were on holy ground, in a place where the veil between the physical world and the spiritual realm was temporarily removed. This was a foreshadowing of His resurrection body, but all it really tells us is that His body was luminous—that is, glorified. Because Jesus Christ is the one person in whom two natures are united—divinity united to humanity—His divine nature glorified His humanity so that, in reality, He didn't need to wait for resurrection for His body to be glorified, since He was without sin and did not need salvation.

Therefore, it is Jesus' Resurrection that gives us the most clues about our own future resurrection body. This is not to say that we can assume that our spiritual bodies will be exactly like Jesus' raised body in every way. We just don't know that for sure. But it's safe to assume that since He is "the first-born from the dead" (that is, the first to experience resurrection; Col. 1:18), and since His Resurrection makes ours possible, there must be some clues about our spiritual body in Jesus' body after the Resurrection. Incidentally, this is why the Church has always insisted that Jesus was raised bodily. His Resurrection is not just a metaphor for "going to Heaven"; He was raised in His whole person, including His body, and if it were not so, then our hope of resurrection would be in vain. As St. Paul said, "If Christ has not been raised, your faith is futile and you are still in your sins" (1 Cor. 15:17).

But when we look at the Gospel accounts of Jesus' Resurrection appearances, we often get conflicting messages. At first, the disciples don't recognize Him (John 20:14–15; 21:4; see also the doubt of some in Matt. 28:17). In the beautiful account of the two disciples on the road to Emmaus (Luke 24:13–35; cf. Mark 16:12), these followers of Jesus listen to Him teach as they walk for miles on the road, but they don't recognize Him until He breaks the bread. On the other hand, when Luke's Gospel tells us that some disciples thought they were seeing a ghost, I take that to mean they *did* recognize Him but, knowing He had died, assumed He was a ghost. This is not a statement about what He looked like, but an acknowledgment that they knew who He was.

On at least one occasion, He didn't want to be touched (John 20:17), and He seemed to be able to walk through walls (John 20:19, 26, and possibly Luke 24:36). At other times, He could be touched, as disciples clung to His feet (Matt. 28:9), and He even encouraged them to touch Him to see that He was tangible (that is, *huggable*; Luke 24:39–40; John 20:24–28). Finally, it's not for nothing that the Gospel writers go out of their way to tell us that Jesus ate after His Resurrection (Luke 24:41–43; see John 21:12–13). Again, this was to emphasize that His Resurrection was not spiritual only, but also physical — that is, He rose bodily. He rose, not only with His body, but also with the wounds from His Passion (John 20:20).

St. Jerome warns us not to take the miraculous nature of the post-Resurrection appearances as any evidence of an ethereal or phantasmal Jesus. He was raised with a solid body, Jerome assures us, and His ability to walk through walls or to inhibit people's ability to recognize Him were functions of the same miraculous power that allowed Him to walk on water before His Passion

(Letter 108, *To Eustochium*). Jerome may be criticizing one or more of his fellow Church Fathers, such as St. John Chrysostom, who seemed to think Jesus' resurrection body was "lacking all density" (Chrysostom, *Homilies on the Gospel of John* 87.1) But Chrysostom is in the minority among Church Fathers, most of whom would reject the idea of an ethereal Jesus. St. Jerome answers those who want to see in the Gospels a spiritualized kind of Resurrection by referring to Jesus' words in Luke 24:39: "See my hands and my feet, that it is I myself; handle me, and see; for a spirit has not flesh and bones as you see that I have." Then Jerome comments: "You hear him speak of bones and flesh, of feet and hands; and yet you want to palm off on me the bubbles and airy nothings of which the Stoics rave!"

At this point, we should not assume that those aspects of Jesus' post-Resurrection nature that we would consider miraculous (such as popping into a locked room) will apply to us in the resurrection life. What we can say is that we will be raised with a solid, tangible body, perfected beyond the reach of sickness or weakness, yet perhaps even retaining some scars from our experiences in this life. But what are we to make of the fact that Jesus was sometimes unrecognizable? We will explore this in more depth in another chapter, but for now it's enough to say that the primary reason Jesus was not recognized was that He did not want to be recognized at first. Ultimately, though, those who loved Him did recognize Him. His body was the same body He had in life, but it was changed in significant ways. And if you're wondering about eating in the heavenly realm, we'll get to that question a little later as well.

Jesus remained on earth, continuing His ministry in His resurrection body, for forty days. The apostles certainly saw and experienced (and hugged) more than they would later write about. So even though the Scriptures don't give us a lot to go on so far, the fact that all of the apostles and the early Church Fathers insisted on the reality of a bodily resurrection of Jesus must mean something. This was not the wishful thinking of a bunch of dreamers. And it could not be a fabricated myth, since there were too many people around who were eyewitnesses to the truth.

At the end of that forty-day period, Jesus ascended to the Father. In other words, He transferred Himself to the spiritual realm. But He did not shed His humanity or slough off His body, like a snake shedding its skin. He entered the spiritual realm with His whole humanity intact, including His body. He exists to this day (and to eternity) with His two natures, divine and human, and His human body exists in the spiritual realm. This is why it's called a spiritual body — because the resurrected body is made ready for the spiritual realm of the Kingdom of Heaven.

But Jesus did not leave us without access to His body here on earth. Every time we receive the Eucharist, we receive the Body and Blood of the Lord. And the Eucharist is not simply a memorial of something that happened 1,986 years ago. It's something that continues to happen now, and continues to bless recipients with grace, because the Body and Blood of Jesus are present not only on the altar — they live even now at the right hand of the Father. You see, all of this is connected. The body of Christ that hung on the Cross *is* the body of Christ that rose from the tomb, *is* the body of Christ that ascended to the Father, and *is* the Body of Christ that is presented on the altar and that makes those who receive it into the Body of Christ, the Church. And this is why we bow and genuflect before the consecrated elements: we are not bowing to statues, icons, or symbols; we bow to the Real

Presence of Christ in His Body and Blood, at the same time both here on earth and in the Kingdom of Heaven. (For more on this, see the chapter on the Eucharist in my book *Handed Down: The Catholic Faith of the Early Christians*.)

3

Yoga, Yoda, and YOLO

Sometimes it doesn't pay to get off the couch. Tony shook his head as he scanned his family, seated in a row of bleachers. They were cold, tired, and hungry. The game he had looked forward to all year long had turned out to be pretty boring, and now, late in the fourth quarter, it was starting to snow. He started thinking about the money he spent on the tickets. *Don't go there*, he told himself. One of his kids said something about having to go to the bathroom, and all of a sudden the other two had to go as well. Tony turned to his brother in the row behind him. "What do you think? Beat the traffic?"

Uncle Rich was smiling and shivering at the same time. Caught off guard, he thought for a moment. "Nah." He looked at his family. They seemed to be happy enough. "Let's stick it out. It's Lambeau!"

But Tony was impatient, and after a short "family meeting," they gathered up their things and shuffled out of their row. Quick goodbyes, a couple of pecks on a couple of cheeks, and Tony and his family disappeared through the gate. Rich smiled at his own family of five still in their seats, shrugged, and then turned his attention back to the game.

As Tony loaded his gang into the minivan, his heart sank as he heard the stadium erupt in cheers. The Packers had scored the winning touchdown.

* * *

Did you recognize that parable? It's the parable of the ten bridesmaids (Matt. 25:1–13). In that parable — another one that begins, "The Kingdom of Heaven is like this ..." — Jesus tells of ten bridesmaids. Five of them are described as wise, and five are described as foolish. All these bridesmaids had to do was wait for the groom to return and be ready when he arrived. But only half of them were smart enough to know that they could not assume that the groom would arrive on their schedule. So, they made a commitment to be in it for the long haul, and brought extra oil for their lamps, so that even if the groom should take a lot longer than they wanted him to, they would be ready. Well, wouldn't you know it, the groom did take longer to return, and by the time he arrived, the lamps were going out. Those who had to go off to buy more oil missed out on the wedding, and the reception.

There's a lot of important teaching packed into this parable. As an analogy, the groom represents Jesus Himself, and the bridesmaids represent those who wait for His return. The second coming of Christ and the resurrection are compared here to a wedding and a wedding reception. Let's keep that in mind for later. For now, I want to point out the fact that the wise people are those who are committed to looking for the return of Christ — they're in it for the long haul — and they are less likely to be distracted from that commitment, even by the necessities of life in the world.

But doesn't it seem as if there is often a struggle within us? Not so much that we are either wise or foolish, but that there are wise and foolish elements within us, wrestling for attention.

We usually know what we should do, but often we are too weak to make the right choice, opting instead for comfort or convenience. Paul recognized this internal struggle when he said, "I do not understand my own actions. For I do not do what I want, but I do the very thing I hate.... I can will what is right, but I cannot do it. For I do not do the good I want, but the evil I do not want is what I do.... I see in my members another law at war with the law of my mind and making me captive to the law of sin which dwells in my members. Wretched man that I am! Who will deliver me from this body of death?" (Rom. 7:15–24).

The Church Fathers followed St. Paul in recognizing a struggle between the physical and the spiritual in us. But let's keep in mind a couple of things before we go any further. First, remember that when Paul says negative things about the body, it's not the body as created by God that he's talking about—it's that tendency toward sin that comes from original sin and now weighs our flesh down. Neither Paul nor the Church Fathers would accept a kind of dualism that says that the body is inherently bad or that evil is a part of creation. That way of thinking is a heresy, commonly called gnosticism, and the Church Fathers rejected it quite aggressively. (For more on the early heresies of docetism and gnosticism, see my books *Reading the Early Church Fathers* and *The Earliest Christologies*.) Finally, this is not a message of despair, and Paul answers his own question in the last verse of that passage: "Who will deliver me from this body of death? Thanks be to God through Jesus Christ our Lord!" (Rom. 7:25).

Body, Mind, and Spirit? (What Is a Human Being Anyway?)
If you've ever gone past a yoga studio, or if you've seen an ad for any kind of new-age spa or Eastern-style therapy, you may

have noticed that they often promise to heal you, "body, mind, and spirit." This is based on what seems to be a kind of popular culture assumption that the human person is made up of these three parts, or aspects: body, mind, and spirit. But is this true?

The Scriptures don't tell us much about what makes up the human person. We know that humanity is created in the image of God (Gen. 1:26–27), but we aren't told exactly what that means. It seems to mean that we are like God in certain ways: God is Love, and we are relational beings, capable of selfless love and compassion; God is Truth, and we are self-aware, rational beings with free will (and moral responsibility for our actions); God is Creator, and we are creative beings capable of bringing order out of chaos, producing art and music simply for the sake of beauty; and God is Spirit, and we are spiritual beings, capable of being in relationship with our Creator, and of being immortal. (For more on the image of God in humanity, see my book *Spiritual Blueprint: How We Live, Work, Love, Play, and Pray*.)

Notice, however, that when we say we are made in the image of God, we are not talking about a physical image. It is not in our bodies that the image of God is found, but in the intangible part of us, whatever that is. Although it's true that sometimes God is described as having body parts (especially in the Old Testament), this is what we call an anthropomorphism—it's a figure of speech whereby we project human qualities onto God to make a point about what God might be doing, but we don't take it literally, as though God has a physical body. To do so would be to make God in *our* image—the exact opposite of what we're talking about!

Remember Bishop Gregory of Nyssa and his conversation with his sister Macrina? In his document containing that conversation, he referred to her as "the Teacher." And she told Gregory that the image of God is the spiritual and intellectual part of a person;

that is, it is not found in the physical parts of a person, but it is immaterial, invisible, and noncorporeal (without dimensions or weight). It is that part of the human that is a kind of microcosm of God—divinity on a smaller scale—with, of course, the caveat that the difference between the two is that the human image is a created thing and the original (God) is uncreated and eternal.

St. Augustine believed that the image of God could be seen in the human person, in an analogy of the Trinity. In his treatise *On the Trinity*, he wrote that the human spirit is made up of memory, intellect, and will, which is an image of the Trinity within us: Father, Son, and Holy Spirit. Not that we should make a direct correlation between the human memory and God the Father, the human intellect and God the Son, and the human will and God the Spirit, but there are some ways in which human understanding is a mirror image of Christ as divine *Word* (that is, rationality), and the human will can be a mirror image of the activity of God in the Holy Spirit. In any case, St. Augustine was affirming what we suspected—the image of God is in the *mind* of a person, not in the body.

For Augustine, the mind is exactly the same thing as what we might call the soul, or the spirit, of a person. But here's where we come to an interesting fork in the road of history. It turns out there is no clear consensus among the Church Fathers as to how many parts a human person has. Some said we are made up of two parts: a body and a soul (which can also be called a spirit). Others said we are made up of three parts, and that the soul and the spirit are different things. For a more in-depth discussion on this topic, see the appendix, "The Human Being: Two Parts or Three?"

For our purposes, it is fair to the witness of the Church Fathers to say either that the spirit and the soul are the same thing or that the spirit is within the soul, and so the two can be thought of as one thing without doing damage to the image of God in humanity. The soul or spirit is the intangible, internal self, which can perceive anything outside the self only through the senses of the body. This means that the body is the soul's interface with the rest of creation. Also, the soul or spirit can move throughout creation and enact its will in the world only through the agency of the body. The point is that the deepest part of the internal self—whether we call it "spirit" or "soul"—is the mind, the intellectual self, which consists of memory, intellect (understanding), and will, and which is that part of the self that mirrors God as His image and is able to communicate with God.[1]

In the rest of this book, the terms "spirit" and "soul" might be used interchangeably (especially in quotations where the Church Fathers may alternate terms) to mean our mind or inner self. For the sake of convenience, however, I prefer to use the term "spirit" to refer to spirit and soul together. It would also be fair simply to use the word "mind" to refer to all of this, since for the Church Fathers, the mind *is* that deepest part of the self, and "mind" is synonymous with "spirit," "rational soul," and even "self" (Augustine, *On the Trinity* 14.16, 15.1).

This means that, in casual conversation, there is nothing wrong with referring to the human being as "mind and body," "body and soul," or "body and spirit." But new-age phrases such as "body, mind, and spirit" are misguided because the mind *is* the spirit. They are also misleading because they imply that the

---

[1]   For more on this concept, see Joseph Ratzinger (Pope Benedict XVI), *Eschatology: Death and Eternal Life* (Washington, D.C.: Catholic University of America Press, 2007), 255–256. Ratzinger's excellent book confirms and informs much of what I am saying in the present book and should be the next place to go for anyone wishing to dig deeper into the doctrine of the resurrection.

mind is something purely intellectual, while the spirit is a different part of us that may connect with the divine, but not on an intellectual level. This is dangerous thinking, because it implies that God is not intellectual (rational) and skews our view of the image of God in us. If one prefers to speak of a three-part human, and one prefers to use the term "mind" for the spirit, then one could say, "body, mind, and soul." But we are still stuck with the problem of an apparent division between that part of us that thinks rationally and that part of us that connects with God, and that just plays into the hands of atheists who want to say that faith in God is not rational.

Therefore, I recommend that when we speak of the human person, we generally stick with the two-part configuration "body and spirit," letting the word "spirit" stand for all that is intangible in us; identity, consciousness, and will, essentially that part of us that we call the mind and is made in the image of God.

The Eternal Connection

In the film *The Empire Strikes Back* (1980), Jedi master Yoda explains the Force to his apprentice, Luke Skywalker. In spite of the fact that the worldview of the *Star Wars* universe is quite gnostic, and therefore dualistic, Yoda (in one of the greatest inconsistencies of the films) tells Luke that the Force is an energy that binds everything together, even mind and matter (for more on the theology of *Star Wars*, see my book *From Star Wars to Superman: Christ Figures in Science Fiction and Superhero Films*). Although, from a Christian perspective, Yoda gets most things wrong, there is one concept that he and the Church Fathers might agree on. The body and mind (spirit) are connected, so much so that they cannot be separated completely, even by death.

What *Really* Happens after We Die

Tertullian wrote that the human body and spirit do not come from separate places to be united. They have no existence apart from each other. Contrary to what some heretics speculated, it is not the case that the human spirit pre-exists the body. Both spirit and body are created together in the womb, at the same moment of conception, and exist only in union (*On the Resurrection of the Flesh* 16, 45, 57). Tertullian says, "Even if we become injured in the womb, this is loss suffered by what is already a human being," a sobering reminder of the humanity of every person from the moment of conception. In *A Treatise on the Soul*, Tertullian points out that the Christian believes that a baby gets his or her spirit at conception, whereas the pagan believes that a baby gets his or her spirit at birth, so that the pagan can say that the baby in the womb is not a person or is not alive before the moment of birth. But Tertullian uses the Gospel account of Mary's visit to Elizabeth, when "the babe leaped in her womb" (Luke 1:41), to demonstrate that both babies were alive before their birth, and to conclude that "life begins at conception." (For more on the connection of dualism and gnosticism with the practice of abortion, see Pope St. John Paul II, *Evangelium Vitae*.)

St. Macrina also taught that the spirit and the body are created together and rejected any idea of the pre-existence of souls as a gnostic teaching. Remember that Jesus Christ is fully human as well as divine. It is not the case that His divine nature "replaced" something in His humanity, as though He were a human body with a divine soul. This would make Him less than fully human, and this idea is a heresy called Apollinarianism (for more on that, see my books *Reading the Early Church Fathers* and *From Star Wars to Superman*). Jesus' divine nature was, in fact, pre-existent (John 1:1), but that divine nature acquired a complete human nature—body *and* spirit (soul and mind) — that was created at the moment of Jesus' conception to be united with His divinity.

So, the human spirit and body are created together and remain together. And when they sin, they sin together. Even though the Church Fathers advised their readers to make the spirit master over the body, they still knew that one could not separate the two when it came to the moral responsibility for one's actions. The second-century Christian philosopher and apologist Athenagoras pointed out that although one might say that we sin with our bodies, it is actually the spirit (the mind) that makes the decisions and drives the actions of the body. Just as an embarrassment in the mind can make the body blush, so some things such as courage require the fear of bodily harm to make the virtue real. Nor can the body put all the blame for sin on the spirit, since no spirit by itself could ever commit adultery. So, it would be unjust of God to hold one accountable and not the other. But the good news, he said, is that since the spirit and the body are so intimately connected, God's intention is for both of them to rise in the end and to be immortal (*On the Resurrection of the Dead*).

Tertullian, too, said that the body cannot do anything without the spirit (the mind) telling it what to do, and the spirit cannot do anything without the agency of the body, so the body cannot be guilty of any sin without the spirit, and the spirit cannot be guilty without the body (*On the Resurrection of the Flesh* 16). Later, around the end of the fourth century, St. Ambrose of Milan (bishop from 374 to 397) wrote that since the body and the spirit cooperate in this life (including in sin), the body and the spirit must be judged together (and if necessary, punished together). And if someone were to enter the Kingdom of Heaven as a spirit only, without a body, that would be only a partial redemption, and the whole person would not be saved (*On the Belief in the Resurrection* 52, 126).

What *Really* Happens after We Die

This led the Church Fathers to feel it necessary to be very clear and very adamant about the fact that it is the *same* body that a person had in life that will be raised and reunited with the spirit in the resurrection. Tertullian said, "Let our own people, moreover, bear this in mind, that souls are to receive back at the resurrection the self-same bodies in which they died" (*A Treatise on the Soul* 56). Macrina taught that, after the death of the body, the spirit watches over the decaying bits, apparently keeping track of all of them for the day when they will be needed again. Even if this is a bit romanticized, as Joseph Ratzinger wrote, "the soul can never completely leave behind its relationship with matter" (Ratzinger, *Eschatology*, p. 179).

St. Ambrose, in *On Belief in the Resurrection*, made what should be an obvious observation. But for a lot of people both then and now, it runs counter to their expectation (and even their hope) for the afterlife. He said that every person is a body fitted to a spirit, and therefore the human person is both parts together. Therefore, even at death, the two parts cannot be completely separated, nor can they be thought of as interchangeable. The same body must be raised and united to the same spirit, because if not, the result would not be the same person. Bishop Rufinus of Aquileia wrote a commentary on the Apostles' Creed, in which he tells his readers that in his diocese, they changed the creed to say, "I believe in … the resurrection of *this flesh*," as a way to emphasize the fact that it would be the same body we have now that will be raised.

You Only Live Once

The author of the Letter to the Hebrews makes an offhand comment that turns out to be significant for our understanding of the apostles' assumptions about the afterlife. In Hebrews 9:27–28,

36

the author is wrapping up a logical proof for why the sacrifice of Christ in His Passion does not need to be repeated. It says, "And just as it is appointed for men to die once, and after that comes judgment, so Christ, having been offered once to bear the sins of many ..." It seems like almost a throwaway line, but in that one verse (27) our apostolic author has just told us that Plato was wrong about the afterlife. So are millions of people today. There is no reincarnation. You die only once.

For those of us who are Christian, we might think this is a no-brainer, but behind this idea, there is a very important point to be made. Not only is it wrong to say that the human body is to be discarded; it is also wrong to say that the human body is interchangeable. Each person's body is an essential part of who he or she is, and to imagine switching bodies (as often happens in science fiction) or to imagine the preservation of a person's mind or consciousness in an artificial medium without a body (whether as a head in a glass jar, as in the old movies, or memories uploaded to a computer, as in the new ones) would result in, at best, the loss of one's personality, and at worst, the complete loss of humanity.

If we take a gnostic approach to personhood and think of the body as simply a shell for the "real" person inside, then we lose an essential aspect of who a person is, and we run the risk of giving ourselves permission to ignore our responsibility to care for the bodies of the poor, the dying, and the dead (for more on the ethical implications of gnosticism, see my book *The Earliest Christologies*). The Church Fathers consistently rejected gnosticism for these reasons, and ultimately this is partly why they always insisted on affirming the doctrine of the resurrection body. Those who say that there was no consensus on this point, or that the concept of the resurrection was an open question in the early Church, are lumping the gnostic heretics in with the mainstream and giving them a credibility they never had and do not deserve.

If the teaching of the Church Fathers on the resurrection is true, then reincarnation cannot be possible. And that makes the idea of the transmigration of souls into animals equally impossible. But this must have been a real question in the time of the early Christians, because virtually all the Church Fathers who wrote on the resurrection felt the need to address the issue. Tertullian, in *A Treatise on the Soul*, chapter 32, said that because the body and the spirit are created together, they are meant to be reunited in the end, and because animals are not made in the image of God, an animal's body cannot house a human spirit. He also said that an animal's body could not house a human spirit because in the case of most animals (and especially bugs) the human spirit would be too big! (This demonstrates that, for the Church Fathers, the human spirit is not "purely" spiritual, i.e., immaterial, the way God is spiritual. See the appendix.)

But for Tertullian, the most important reason why reincarnation and the transmigration of souls is impossible is that it would make judgment impossible: How could anyone be judged for his or her actions if one person's spirit goes into another body? The sins of any person's life are accountable to both body and spirit. The point is that the concept of reincarnation is not compatible with Christian teaching—not just because of one verse in Hebrews, but because it would contradict our whole concept of personhood, judgment, and the afterlife.

Macrina also (through Gregory of Nyssa) taught that a person's body and spirit are so united that a spirit cannot trade one body for another, especially not the body of an animal. One body is all any spirit gets. St. Ambrose of Milan understood that the concept of transmigration assumes that animals have spirits (rational souls), which contradicts the Christian doctrine that only human spirits are created in the image of God. What would happen, he snarked, if a bird's soul were to enter into a human body? Would it be sad that it could no longer fly? Maybe the reason Icarus tried to fly too close to the sun was that in a past life he had been a bird! No, said Ambrose, "The work of God does not perish.... Those who are made in the image of God cannot be transformed into the shapes (natures) of beasts; since in truth it is not the form (nature) of the body but of the spirit which is made after the likeness of God" (*On Belief in the Resur-rection* 129). In any case, if you think God can put the spirit of one person into another's body, you should believe that it's even easier for God to put the spirit of a person back into his or her own body (*On Belief in the Resurrection* 65). And that is exactly what we believe that God will do.

The point of all this is that because we believe that the human spirit (including the mind and the will) is made in the image of God, human beings are completely different from animals, espe-cially in terms of our relationship with God. The proof of this, for the Church Fathers, is that we do not breed with animals (it would be impossible if we tried), but we do eat animals. We can only form families with other humans (yes, I know your dog is part of the family, but that's not what I mean), and we are not allowed to eat our fellow humans. Some vegetarians will say that we shouldn't eat animals, either, and that's their choice, but as history demonstrates, the danger of assuming that humans and animals are essentially the same is that, sooner or later, you stop treating animals like people and start treating people like ani-mals. The image of God in us means that all humans are created equal, but animals are not created to be equal to humans (see St. Augustine, *On Faith and the Creed* 4).

This brings us to ask the question: What, then, is it to be human? In other words, if we are coming to the conclusion that the body cannot be discarded or traded for another because each person's body is integral to who he or she is, then what else is essential to the person (and what is not)? First, let's sort out some things that are not part of the essence of humanity.

Following on some of St. Paul's teachings about the struggle between the spirit and the flesh, the Church Fathers maintained that although the body is essential to the human, the *desires* of the flesh are not. Certainly, any desires that cause us to sin are not part of who we really are. In fact, it is important to point out that sin is not a part of humanity. In other words, humanity was created to be without sin, and therefore sin is not part of the essence of what it means to be human.

I have heard people say that they believe that Jesus sinned because they reasoned that if He did not sin, He would not be truly human. It should go without saying that Jesus was without sin (Heb. 4:15). But for someone to say that Jesus "had to" sin if He was fully human is to assume that sin is an essential part of what it means to be human. But this is not true. As humans, we were meant to be without sin, so that when Jesus, in His human life, was able to avoid sin, He was living up to the potential of humanity more than anyone. He was actually *more* fully human than we are, because when we sin, we fall short of our full humanity. Never let anyone tell you that Jesus had to sin to be human. To sin is to be inhuman.

In addition to the desires that cause us to sin, even the acceptable desires that keep us alive in the physical world are not essential parts of our humanity. This is because desires are based on need, and in the afterlife, there is no need. As St. Paul said in 1 Corinthians 6:13, "'Food is meant for the stomach and the stomach for food'—and God will destroy both one and the other." We'll come back to the question of eating in Heaven, but for now, the point is that in the afterlife we won't need to eat or drink to survive, so we won't need desires such as hunger or thirst. We also apparently won't have sexual desire, because there will be no need to procreate, which is Jesus' point in the passage about living like angels, quoted above. And it goes without saying that in Heaven nature never calls.

Macrina explained to her brother Gregory that many of our emotions are also not essential to our humanity and will not exist in the afterlife. All of the Church Fathers would agree, and this could be chalked up to the influence of Stoicism on the Roman mind (make sure your reason rules over your emotions because emotions can't be trusted). But it makes sense when we realize that many emotions are based on situations that simply won't exist in the next life. There will be no need for fear, when danger is no more. And there won't even be a need for faith or hope, when we have been welcomed into the presence of God and received what we hope for (see 1 Cor. 13:13; Heb. 11:1). To the extent that love is an emotion, it will, of course, continue to exist into eternity, but love is so much more than an emotion, and any love we have is sustained on the foundation of the love of God, who *is* love.

We have already acknowledged that the body is essential to what it means to be human, but we must not read into this that certain physical attributes are integral to our identity. In other words, your skin color is not an essential part of your humanity, any more than your hair color or eye color is (see St. Augustine, *On the Trinity* 5.7, 7.1). When we talk about what is essential to our humanity, we are talking about aspects that all humans share in common, not characteristics that divide us, such as ethnicity or language. The essence of humanity is what the Divine Word took on in the Incarnation to become like all of us, so it cannot be anything that some of us have and others don't. If it were, Christ would not be one of us in our human totality (that is, He would be like only some of us), and we could not all be saved by Him. What connects us to Him is precisely what connects us to each other—all of us, all of humanity. There is far too much division among us, and far too many of us define our identities by things that divide us. It is time we begin to define ourselves by what we share in common. We are embodied spirits, created in the image of God, with the capacity for love, compassion, reason, and creativity. This is what we have in common, with each other, and with Christ.

Having said that, I have to point out that although we will not have sexual desire or marriage in the kingdom (Mark 12:25; Luke 20:34-36), Pope St. John Paul II, in his *Theology of the Body*, has clarified that we will retain our identity as males or females. Masculinity or femininity are particular to our individual bodies, so that even though the Church Fathers liked to quote Jesus saying that we will be like angels in our heavenly celibacy, that does not mean that we will become androgynous or even asexual beings. I would still say that our maleness or femaleness is not an essential part of our *humanity*—that is, what makes us human—since Christ came as a man but still shares the same humanity with women, but our maleness or femaleness is apparently a part of our individual personality, and so will be retained in the resurrection body.

So then, what *is* a human being? What is essential to the human person? Who am I at the core of my being? Another way to ask this question is to ask: What survives physical death? What parts of me "go to Heaven"? When we talk about salvation, what is it that is redeemed?

First, we have to remember, as all the Church Fathers and Mothers taught, that at the moment of physical death, the spirit leaves the body, and the body dies (see St. Augustine, *On the Trinity* 4.3, and Ratzinger, *Eschatology*, p. 258). The body cannot live without the spirit, and the moment it's gone, the body begins to decay. So, the spirit can live without the body, but the body cannot live without the spirit. And for the time between an individual's death and the resurrection, the spirit and the body are separated. The spirit goes on to the spiritual realm, but the body is not yet suited to the spiritual realm and it stays behind on earth, where it begins to break down into its smaller parts. (Incidentally, we can't assume the same about Jesus. Since He was without sin, His body would not have suffered the effects of sin, which include corruption. So, for the day and a half that His spirit was separated from His body, His body was truly dead but did not begin to decay.) We'll talk about this interim time in another chapter—the point for now is that this is not the end of the story. Since the body and the spirit were created together, they are meant to be together, and they must be reunited at some point. This is the resurrection.

What is raised is what is redeemed, and that is the essence of the human being. The human person is body and spirit together, even though the body and the spirit are separated for a time. The reason Plato and others are wrong about reincarnation is that an individual's body is essential to who that person is, and as the Church Fathers and Mothers taught, it must be the same body the person had in life, or it's not the same person. This becomes especially clear when we remember that in life our bodies are temples of the Holy Spirit (1 Cor. 6:19). If we do not want to lose our identity in the afterlife, we cannot lose our body either. Anything less would fail to redeem the whole person (Ratzinger, *Eschatology*, pp. 172, 175).

The resurrection, then, is a reunion of body and spirit, a return to the way a person is supposed to be, but without being weighed down with things such as sin and fear, which are not meant to be part of the human experience (Heb. 12:1–2). It is not the case that death is an escape from the "prison" of the body, as if the spirit is meant to be without a body. The idea of the afterlife as a disembodied spirit is not a Christian concept — it is pagan, and gnostic. When the Scriptures and the Church Fathers speak of the "resurrection of the flesh," they mean the resurrection of the whole person, spirit with body reunited (Ratzinger, *Eschatology*, p. 176).

In Gregory of Nyssa's *On the Soul and the Resurrection*, St. Macrina gives us a definition of "resurrection." She says that it is "the reconstitution of our nature in its original form ... [that is, as our nature was before the Fall, when] there was neither age nor infancy, nor any of the sufferings arising from our present various infirmities, nor any kind of bodily affliction whatever." We should not go too far in speculation about what humanity was like before the Fall, since there is no consensus about this among the Church Fathers and Mothers. Nevertheless, Macrina (and Gregory) believed that in the resurrection, we will be restored to the innocence, peace, and health that humanity was created to enjoy before it felt the effects of sin. They believed that before the sin of Adam and Eve, humanity was in a state of grace, in which the human body was incorrupt. Therefore, the resurrection body will also be incorrupt, sin and suffering having no part of the Kingdom of Heaven.

The essence of who we are as humans is what we were created to be—spirits created in the image of God that interact with creation through strong, healthy bodies. Keep in mind that even Heaven is created, so, although it may be outside of physical space, and may even be outside of linear time, it is still "material," in the sense that it is something other than God Himself. So, in order to interface with our environment in the heavenly realm, and to interact with other people, we will still need bodies to receive information through the senses and to enact our wills. Those bodies, having been raised and glorified, will be spiritual bodies, changed to be suited to the spiritual realm, but they will still be bodies.

To say that the resurrection body is a spiritual body does not mean that it is an intangible body, for that really would be a contradiction in terms. Our spiritual bodies will be solid, with mass and dimensions of size—they will take up space. To say anything else is to fall into the trap of that spirit-matter dualism. Notice that we are told in the book of Revelation that angels have physical size (the same size as humans; Rev. 21:17). They, too, have spiritual bodies, though of a different kind from what ours will be. But we will be like angels, Jesus tells us, because our resurrection bodies, like theirs, will be *both* matter and spirit. And our bodies, though changed, will still be consistent with the bodies that housed our spirits on earth, since anything less would mean the loss of our identities.

In the afterlife, we will not be absorbed into the universe, and we will not leave our personalities behind. Being made in the image of God means that our agency, our creativity, our relationships, our minds and memories, even our sense of humor, will all be retained. These are the things that survive physical death, and these are the things that make us who we are. And although we each have our own unique version of these things, it is the fact that we have them that makes us one human race and unites us to each other.

Jesus' parable of the ten bridesmaids is an allegory of the Church waiting for the return of Christ, when the resurrection will take place. Christ is the Groom, and the Church is His Bride (Eph. 5:23–27). And just as any bride would prepare herself in a special way for her wedding day, our bodies will also be prepared by being glorified and transformed into spiritual bodies, to be suited to the spiritual realm in the Kingdom of Heaven.

4

God's Jigsaw Puzzle

Sarah loved tulips. Every picture that came home from kindergarten was a picture of tulips. She used every crayon in the box. Everyone knew that tulips were Sarah's favorite flower, and if you didn't know that, she made sure to tell you within thirty seconds of meeting her. The spring Sarah turned six, her auntie gave her a present for Easter. It was a tulip bulb. Auntie told Sarah that if she planted it in the garden, a beautiful tulip would grow.

But Sarah didn't want to plant it in the garden. She remembered what happened to Whiskers. They buried her in the garden. And boy, were her parents mad when she dug up her beloved cat! Sarah knew she would remember for the rest of her life the sight she saw when she opened that box. And she did not want that to happen to her new tulip bulb. So she cherished that tulip bulb — not because it was beautiful in itself, but because, to her, it represented all tulips. Sarah took her pretty lace handkerchief and lovingly wiped the dust off the bulb. She took the trays out of her jewelry box and put the tulip bulb in the box. And every day she opened the jewelry box and took the tulip bulb out and held it in her hands.

After a while, every day turned into once a week, and then Sarah forgot about the tulip bulb in her jewelry box — that is, until one day when she heard her mother screaming from her room, "Sarah!"

When Auntie found out, she was visibly disappointed that Sarah had not planted the bulb in the garden. She took Sarah's little hands in hers, looked her in the eyes, and said, "Sarah, honey. Don't you know that a tulip bulb can never become the beautiful tulip that it was meant to be unless you let it go, let it get dirty, even let it break apart in the earth, so the flower can come out?"

* * *

Jesus said, "Truly, truly, I say to you, unless a grain of wheat falls into the earth and dies, it remains alone; but if it dies, it bears much fruit" (John 12:24). When Jesus said this, He had just made a reference to His own coming death. The point, I think, is that this is one of the times when He was preparing His disciples for the fact that it was His mission to die. But then He went on to say that anyone who clings to this life risks losing eternal life, and anyone who is willing to let go of life on earth for the sake of following Christ will receive eternal life.

I Believe in . . . the Resurrection of the Body

For the apostles and the Church Fathers, the real flesh and blood of Jesus is important, because, without it, Jesus didn't really become truly human. And if He didn't become one of us, then how could He die for us, as one of us? In other words, how could He be the Savior of humanity if He was not human? This is why the Church Fathers argued so adamantly against docetism (dualism) and gnosticism (for more on the apostles' and Church Fathers' arguments for Jesus' real humanity, see my books *Reading the Early Church Fathers, Trinity 101*, and *The Earliest Christologies*). In fact, several of the Church Fathers had a version of this saying: *Whatever is not assumed is not saved.* If the Savior did not assume (take on) humanity, then He could not save humanity. He could save only what He became, because, according to the justice of God, it had to be a human who paid for the sins of humanity.

The apostles and the Church Fathers also knew that when Jesus was raised, He was raised bodily. His Resurrection was not just some metaphorical way of describing that He had transcended this life. He could be touched, and He could eat. Furthermore, Jesus said that He would raise us up "on the last day" (see John 6:40), so as the apostles and the Church Fathers reflected on the Resurrection of Jesus, they were convinced that we would follow in Christ's Resurrection, that we, too, would be raised—not simply "go to Heaven" in a noncorporeal way, but we would be raised bodily, as Jesus was.

In the second century, the Christian philosopher Justin Martyr asked: Why would He rise—and ascend—in the flesh, if not to show us that we will also rise in the flesh? (This is in the existing fragments of *On the Resurrection*, though we have to admit that scholars are not absolutely sure that Justin Martyr wrote this document.) The conviction of the Church has always been that our bodies must participate in our salvation; otherwise a part of who we are would not be saved (and for some of the Church Fathers, the body was the very part that had done most of the sinning and needs redemption the most). Again, Justin Martyr asks: If Christ came to save only the soul, how is this any different from what Plato and the other pagan philosophers said? So, if God does not raise the body, then He has not redeemed the whole person. As Tertullian said, "Does it happen that, when you now admit the salvation of only the soul, you ascribe it to men at the cost of half their nature?" (*On the Resurrection of the Flesh* 57).

Clearly Jesus saw the redemption of the body as important, since a major part of His ministry was the healing of bodies. He was not just a philosopher who said wise things that appealed to the mind. He was a healer, because God cares about our bodies too. Jesus was concerned for making the body whole in this life, so of course He would be interested in the ultimate healing of the person—a salvation in which both spirit and body are raised and redeemed, and in which both mind and body are healed, perfected, and glorified.

When St. Paul was asked, "How are the dead raised? With what kind of body do they come?" (1 Cor. 15:35), he began to explain what we should think of this "spiritual body," or what we often call the "resurrection body." And when we look carefully at what he said, and at how the Church Fathers (and Mothers) interpreted the teachings of the apostles on this point, we can see that we should not think of eternal life as a disembodied existence.

However, we also can see from the early Church writings that some must have objected to this idea by quoting Paul's comment in 1 Corinthians 15:50: "I tell you this, brethren: flesh and blood cannot inherit the kingdom of God, nor does the perishable inherit the imperishable." What about that? Well, we know that when Paul talks about "flesh," he often means the sinful desires of the flesh that are not part of the essence of humanity, and that do not survive death. Tertullian would point out that this passage could not mean that the Kingdom is a disembodied ex-istence, because we know that it is possible for a body to exist in Heaven—Jesus' body exists there "at the right hand of God the

Father," ever since His Ascension. (Tertullian, in *On the Flesh of Christ* 16, and *On the Resurrection of the Flesh* 51). So, Christ exists bodily in the heavenly realm even now. Although St. Paul says that "the perishable does not inherit the imperishable," the fact is that in our resurrection, God will not raise perishable bodies: He will raise glorified bodies that have been transformed to become imperishable (Tertullian, *On the Resurrection of the Flesh* 32, 57). Paul himself goes on to say, in the very next verse, "I tell you a mystery. We shall not all sleep, but we shall all be changed" (1 Cor. 15:51). In the resurrection, our bodies will be changed from corruption to incorruption (Justin Martyr, *On Resurrection* 4, 10, and *1 Apology* 19, 52).

St. Augustine said that the resurrection body is *not* flesh and blood at all, but something else (*On Faith and the Creed* 10). It will be an "uncorrupted and very light body" but still a body (*On Christian Doctrine* 1.24). Augustine implied that it changed from a fleshly body to a spiritual body, and that's why Paul could say that flesh and blood would not inherit the Kingdom of Heaven. Augustine explained that what Paul mean by the "spiritual body" is that it will be "adapted to a heavenly habitation, all frailty and every earthly blemish having been changed and converted into heavenly purity and stability" (*On Faith and the Creed* 6). This is another example of different authors working with different definitions of the word "flesh," but the point is that Paul's statement does not mean we leave our bodies behind. For St. Augustine, the meaning of a "spiritual body" is a body that submits to the spirit (whereas, in the present life, the body often refuses to submit to the spirit [*City of God* 13.20, 22.21]).

So when we put all this together, we can see that we *will* have bodies in the Kingdom of Heaven, and whatever the "spiritual body" is, it is not an oxymoron—it is not a "noncorporeal body." Although the resurrection body is spiritual—that is, suited for the spiritual realm—it is nevertheless still material and physical. It is tangible (huggable) and it has physical dimensions of size. So, we should not imagine our existence in the heavenly realm as though we are living on some ethereal plane where we wisp around, moving through each other, tiptoeing over the clouds but unable to touch anything. We may think of Heaven as another dimension, but we must not think of it as dimensionless.

Putting It Back Together

It seems that another major objection from the pagan philosophers was the question of how a body could be raised after it had been buried and decayed. And just like the question of reincarnation, virtually all the Church Fathers who write about resurrection chime in on this question. When we read their answers, we find that, although they didn't know the modern science of cells and molecules, they did believe that all matter was made up of smaller, invisible particles they called "atoms." They also assumed the conservation of matter, meaning that they did not believe any of these atoms could simply be annihilated into nothingness—they all had to go somewhere. Nothing really "goes away"; it only breaks down into its smallest parts. So, the Church Fathers knew that even when a human body decays, the smallest bits into which it could break down were still preserved. And these "atoms" could be put back together by the God who created them in the first place. If God put the human body together, He can surely put it back together. Because Jesus has promised, "Not a hair of your head will perish" (Luke 21:18; cf. St. Augustine, *City of God* 22.21).

Justin Martyr wrote:

> The body itself ... is dissolved again into those atoms from
> which it was also produced. And as these remain indestruc-
> tible, it is not at all impossible, that by coming together
> again, and receiving the same arrangement and position,
> they should make a body of like nature to what was for-
> merly produced by them—as if a jeweler should make in
> mosaic the form of an animal, and the stones should be
> scattered by time, or by the man himself who made them,
> he having still in his possession the scattered stones, may
> gather them together again, and having gathered, may
> dispose them in the same way, and make the same form of
> an animal. And shall not God be able to collect again the
> decomposed members of the flesh, and make the same body
> as was formerly produced by Him? (*On the Resurrection* 6)

Justin says the human body is like a mosaic (a mosaic is a picture made from small colored tiles, which have the effect of pixels
when seen from a distance). Since God is the one who first created
the mosaic (and in His own image, no less), He can certainly put
the tiles back in the right place if they should get scrambled by
the decomposition of the body. Another way to think of this is
like a jigsaw puzzle. If God is the one who made the puzzle, surely
He can put it back together if the pieces get jumbled.

Athenagoras also wrote a document on the resurrection (we're
not entirely certain about the authorship of this document, either,
but whoever wrote it was clearly reading Justin Martyr's treatise
on this topic and expanding upon it). He begins by saying that
nothing is impossible for God. So, to object to the concept of a
resurrection body by saying that it would be impossible to put the
body back together is absurd. God is the Creator. If He can create

bodies from scratch, then it's not difficult for Him to put them back together from their parts. Later Tertullian would continue this same idea by saying:

> For if God produced all things whatever out of nothing, He will be able to draw forth from nothing even the flesh which had fallen into nothing.... Surely the one who created is most competent to re-create, inasmuch as it is a far greater work to have produced than to have reproduced, to have imparted a beginning than to have maintained a continuance. On this principle, you may be quite sure that the restoration of the flesh is easier than its first formation. (*On the Resurrection of the Flesh*)

Just as Tertullian was a disciple of Justin Martyr and Athenagoras on this subject, the Roman apologist Minucius Felix was a disciple of Tertullian. In a document called the *Octavius* (probably written in the early third century), he said that every body that is "dissolved" (decomposed) may seem to us as if it has ceased to exist, but to God it still exists in its basic elements. As the sun, after it has set, does not cease to exist, but is only hidden from us until it rises again; and as the plants that seem to die in the fall but come back in the spring; or the seeds planted in the ground that appear to rot in the earth until a plant emerges; so it is with the human body in the grave — the resurrection is the dawn, or the springtime, of the body. This, Felix explains, is why Christians do not cremate their dead. To do so would be to show a lack of faith in what is to come. In fact, it has been only within the last several decades that the Catholic Church has allowed cremation, though it is still discouraged.

St. Ambrose, too, wrote of the resurrection of the body in comparison to the rising of the sun and the growth of seeds. By looking at nature, he says, we can see that there are cycles of life, death, and resurrection all around us, and the lesson we learn from this is that it is only when a seed gives up its life that the plant can bear fruit. So we should not be surprised that it works this way with people too. It is not that the body has been destroyed by death and decay, but that it has entered into the necessary cycle of life that leads to resurrection (Ambrose of Milan, *On Belief in the Resurrection* 53–54, 60–61, 64). Ambrose wrote, "If God made all these things out of nothing ... why should we wonder that something which once was should be brought to life again, since we see produced that which had not been?"

But what if a person's body is eaten by an animal? The "atoms" of that person's body would then become part of the basic elements of the animal's body, wouldn't they? Or perhaps even worse: they would become part of the animal's feces! As you might guess, the Church Fathers were unfazed by this line of reasoning as well, though they did feel the need to address it. Athenagoras said it's still no problem for God to put all the pieces back together. St. Ambrose answered this objection by saying that every living thing comes from the earth and returns to the earth anyway, so why should we be surprised that God can reconstitute a human body, even when its elements have become part of an animal (and since animals are not raised, the atoms will not be needed for the animal's body). Even in the case of people lost at sea, the sea regularly gives up its dead when bodies wash up on shore, and this is just a foreshadowing of the way in which the earth will give up its dead at the resurrection. (*On Belief in the Resurrection* 55, 58, 64; see also Revelation 20:13).

But what if a person is eaten by another person? Well, as Athenagoras pointed out, this is exactly why cannibalism is off limits for humans. We are not allowed to eat the flesh of other humans, because they are created in the image of God, and their bodies are meant to be redeemed and raised just like ours. Some of the Church Fathers speculated that God prevents human parts from becoming part of another human, or even of animals. They said that even if a human is eaten by another human, human flesh will not nourish a human, but will only pass through and will never become part of the eater. St. Augustine said that the eaten parts of a human are only "borrowed" by the eater and will return to the eaten person at the resurrection (*City of God* 22.20). But whether they agreed with Augustine on this point or not, all the Church Fathers agreed that none of these objections could raise any serious doubt over the bodily resurrection of believers, since, at the end of the day, God is omnipotent, and the Creator has the power to re-create.

The Same but Changed

We have noted that St. Macrina and others taught that there was an eternal connection between a person's spirit and his or her body and that this means that the spirit could never inhabit any other body. Macrina said that the spirit watches over the pieces of the body until they can be reunited in the resurrection. The concept is not so far-fetched, since physicists now speak of "quantum entanglement," a situation in which particles that are connected maintain their connection, even when separated by great distances. Speaking of this same connection of an individual's spirit with his or her body, Tertullian wrote:

> The flesh, indeed, is washed, in order that the soul may be cleansed; the flesh is anointed, that the soul may be consecrated; the flesh is signed (with the cross), that the

soul too may be fortified; the flesh is shadowed with the imposition of hands, that the soul may be illuminated by the Spirit; the flesh feeds on the body and blood of Christ, that the soul likewise may fatten on God. (*On the Resurrection of the Flesh* 8)

In other words, when we participate in the sacraments, not only do the rites affect our bodies, but by presenting our bodies to receive the sacraments, our spirits benefit as well.

In fact, some of the Church Fathers speculated that decay might be necessary, as a kind of purification for the spiritual realm, as if the body is purified by decomposition, while the spirit is purified separately in Purgatory (see Tertullian, *A Treatise on the Soul* 53). This idea may be in conflict with other more prevalent ideas, such as the conviction that the decay of the body is a result of the corruption of sin, but if you think about it, there are saints whose bodies remain incorrupt because their souls were so pure. Could it be that their bodies are more ready for the spiritual realm than the rest of us? Certainly many Church Fathers would advocate living now as we will live in Heaven to prepare ourselves for eternal life. In any case, all the Church Fathers would agree that the resurrection is a perfecting of the body, in one sense restoring it to the way it was meant to be before the Fall, and in another sense, bringing it to the perfection of its potential. In that perfection, there will be no more illness or suffering, and certainly no more death (Rev. 21:4).

As we've noted, the resurrection body must be the same body that a person had in life, otherwise it would not be the same person after the resurrection. But at the same time, the body we know in this life is not suited to the spiritual realm. It is now a "fleshly" or "natural" body, but it will be raised a spiritual body.

This is a bit of a paradox, but it is not a contradiction. It is the same body, in the sense that my body will still be my body, but it will be changed. The two metaphors of mosaic (jigsaw puzzle) and seed and plant are complementary—the metaphor of the mosaic reminds us that it is the same body we had in life that is reconstituted and raised; and the metaphor of the seed and plant reminds us that this body is also re-created when it is redeemed—that is, it is changed. And so, each metaphor corrects possible misunderstandings in the other.

The fact that "flesh and blood cannot inherit the Kingdom of God" and the perishable cannot inherit the imperishable (1 Cor. 15:50) means that the resurrection body cannot be *identical* to the bodies we inhabit now (see Ratzinger, *Eschatology*, p. 160). The resurrection is not simply a resuscitation, such as we see with the child raised by Elijah (1 Kings 17:22), the child raised by Elisha (2 Kings 4:34; 13:21), Lazarus (John 11:1–44), the widow's son (Luke 7:11–17), Jairus's daughter (Mark 5:38–43), and Tabitha (Acts 9:40). Although the Church Fathers mentioned all of these as precedents of the resurrection, they knew that Lazarus and the others would eventually die again. Pope Benedict XVI (when he was Cardinal Ratzinger) said that even the Pharisees' belief in resurrection was more of a belief in resuscitation, since they thought the body of the deceased would rise identical to the way it was when the person died.

On the other hand, the resurrection cannot be that of a *different* body any more than it could be simply a spiritualized metaphor for something disembodied. To be embodied is what is natural to us as humans, and so our embodied nature does not simply "go away" (Ratzinger, *Eschatology*, p. 170). So, the way we should think of the reality of the resurrection is neither the "naturalistic" view of the resuscitation of the identical body, nor the "spiritualistic" view of a disembodied soul. Our spiritual body is the same body, but changed. It is this "middle way" view that embraces the mystery of the paradox, while affirming the reality of both the continuity of the body and the transformation of the body.

At the resurrection, when, as St. Paul says, the last trumpet will sound (1 Cor. 15:52; 1 Thess. 4:16; see Rev. 11:15–19), "we shall be changed." At that time, the body once suited to earth will not only be put back together but will be remade to be suited to the heavenly realm. What was once a "natural body" will become a spiritual body. What was once perishable will become imperishable. What was once mortal will become immortal. What was once corrupt, dishonorable, and weak will rise incorrupt, glorified, and perfected in strength (1 Cor. 15:42–55).

Pope Benedict XVI warns us that this language of the perishable *becoming* the imperishable may imply an oversimplification of the process, even if some of the Church Fathers did use it. Notice that St. Paul says that "this perishable nature must *put on* the imperishable and this mortal nature must *put on* immortality." Perhaps it would be helpful here to think about the Incarnation. When John tells us that the Word *became* flesh (John 1:14), he is not saying that the divine nature of Jesus *turned into* the humanity of Jesus. He is saying that the divine nature of Jesus *came to exist as a human* (without being any less divine). In the same way, our present perishable and mortal bodies will come to exist as imperishable and immortal, without changing into something they were not before. And so, Paul concludes, "O death, where is your victory? O death, where is your sting?" (see 1 Cor. 15:55; see Hosea 13:14). Death itself—the enemy of the body—will be defeated. Death will be dead when the body is raised to life.

At this point, there are certain questions that understandably come up. For example, we know that Jesus' resurrection body still showed the wounds of His Crucifixion. In fact, it seems from the encounter with Thomas (John 20:26–28) that what Thomas touched were still open wounds. The Church Fathers believed that Jesus' wounds were still open and unhealed (see, for example, Gregory of Nyssa, *On the Making of Man* 25.12, and John Chrysostom, *Homilies on the Gospel of John* 87.1), and even Christian art usually depicts Thomas putting his finger *into* Jesus' side. What are we to make of this? Will those of us who suffered in our bodies or who lost limbs (or were born without them) be restored in the resurrection?

Here we have to be careful about two problematic assumptions. First, even though we believe that Jesus is the prototype of our resurrection, we cannot automatically assume that our resurrection will be like His in every way. Second, we have to check our assumptions about what we believe are the criteria for a "normal" or normative body. We do not want to assume that we know what is God's ideal for a "perfect" (or even "in shape") body. Having said that, the Church Fathers seemed to believe that, in the resurrection, our bodies will not only be unsusceptible to illness and injury but will be healed of all past injury (see, for example, Tertullian, *On the Resurrection of the Flesh* 57).

In the *City of God*, St. Augustine wrote that the resurrection body will be repaired of all injuries, deformities, and even blemishes. If someone lost a limb, it will be returned to him. If someone was born without a particular part, then the rule that "beauty is symmetry" applies, and his resurrection body will be supplied with whatever was missing. If a person has an extra appendage, the substance that made up that appendage will not be lost — it will be absorbed into the whole of the body — but the deformity will be gone. Even someone who feels he is too overweight or too skinny will have the shape he wishes he could have now. We will all be raised, St. Augustine said, in whatever size is appropriate for the "flower of youth" (*City of God* 22.19–20). Just as Jesus Christ was the "unblemished Lamb," He will raise His own people unblemished as well (1 Pet. 1:19; see Eph. 5:27).

On the other hand, St. Augustine also said that the martyrs will retain the scars of their sacrifice as marks of honor. They will still receive back any limbs lost, and St. Augustine implies that, unlike Jesus' resurrection body, theirs will not have open wounds, but their scars will be eternal symbols of their ultimate commitment of faith and of God's healing power.

What about age? At what age will our bodies be raised? At the same age we died, or at some ideal age? The Church Fathers rejected the idea that we would be raised at the same age at which we died, since that would mean that there would be babies (including the preborn) in the Kingdom of Heaven. They did not have a consensus on what age might be the ideal age for resurrection, though some speculated that we would all be raised at the same age that Jesus was at His Resurrection (see Jerome, Letter 108, *To Eustochium*). But before you start thinking that the age of thirty-three has a nice Trinitarian ring to it, remember that our present calendars are off by at least four years, so that by our best math, Jesus was actually born in about 4 or 5 B.C. That means that when He was raised from the dead, He was really about thirty-eight years old. The best we can say is probably to go back to St. Augustine's comment about the "flower of youth" and assume that age *as a number* is less the point than the fact that we will feel as if we are in the prime of life.

Finally, while Pope St. John Paul II has assured us that we will retain our maleness or femaleness in the kingdom, there were some in the time of the early Church who wondered whether we will still have genitals. There were a few Church Fathers who were influenced by the heretic Origen (who had castrated himself in an overzealous attempt to live the angelic life in the here and now), who said that our resurrection bodies will not have genitals, but most of the Church Fathers seem to have believed that the parts of our bodies that make us male or female will still be there (see St. Jerome, Letter 84 and 108, *To Eustochium*, and St. Augustine, *Sermon 243*). This may seem like a trivial point, or even one that is beneath the dignity of this conversation, but remember that it was the gnostics who said that our bodies are evil and procreation is bad, and those in the early Church who were led to say that all sexuality is sinful were either too influenced by the gnostics (like Origen) or were driven to extremes by overreacting against them (like Clement of Alexandria).

St. Ambrose pointed out that if God can change an inanimate object into a living creature, as he did when he changed Moses' staff into a serpent (Exod. 4:3), then it is no difficult thing for Him to take a lifeless body and make it live again. If God can take disjointed and broken bodies in the valley of dry bones and pull them together to live again, as He did through Ezekiel (Ezek. 37:1–14), then surely He can raise our bodies to reunite them with our spirits. If Jesus' death could open the tombs and raise the bodies of people who lived before Him (Matt. 27:50–53), then it can certainly do the same for us. And so death is not a release from the "prison" of the body, and it is not a disembodied existence. As Tertullian said, "In Platonic phrase, indeed, the body is a prison, but in the apostles' it is the temple of God" (*A Treatise on the Soul* 53). How could the body be a prison for our spirit, when it is a temple of the Holy Spirit? No, in the Kingdom of God, we will have a bodily existence, and so the idea of hugs in Heaven is at least possible.

5

The Butterfly Effect

The old car had been in the front yard for years. Every time Alan passed it, or even saw it, he felt as if it were mocking him. He had to get that car up and running again. After all, it was his dad's car, and Dad was gone now. But the engine was shot. There was no way that car was ever going to run again without a new engine. So, Alan started saving up for a new engine. He set up an automatic transfer into a savings account to put a little money aside every month. But then he forgot about it for a while. Eventually, when he looked at the account balance, he had enough money for a new engine, and then some.

Alan went online and surfed around awhile, checking prices and models. When all was said and done, he had spent the whole amount in his savings account and had purchased a brand-new Corvette engine. The only problem was, the car in the front yard was not a Corvette; it was an old Volvo. But he was sure he could make it work. And he did. It took some doing, but Alan mounted that new Corvette engine in the old Volvo. And after a lot of tinkering, he got it running. The neighbors shook their heads as he revved the new engine and the old chassis vibrated. The only thing left to do was take it out on the road.

What *Really* Happens after We Die

Alan woke up in a hospital bed. As his eyes strained to focus, he squinted to see a doctor looking at a clipboard. "What ..." Alan's voice cracked. "What happened?"

The doctor shrugged her shoulders. "You put a new engine into an old car. Now they're both wrecked. You're lucky to be alive."

* * *

Jesus said, "No one puts new wine into old wineskins; if he does, the wine will burst the skins, and the wine is lost, and so are the skins; but new wine is for fresh skins" (Mark 2:22; see Matt. 9:17; Luke 5:37–38). When Jesus said this, He was justifying why His disciples were not fasting while He was with them. He was implying that God was doing something new in the Incarnation, and the new covenant will require some new practices. And when it comes to the resurrection, God is not just doing something new: He is making something new—that is, He is re-creating or remaking us for eternal life.

We've been talking about how God will redeem the human body by re-creating, or transforming, it. But it's not only the body that is made new; it's also the human spirit (soul). In fact, it is precisely *because* the spirit is renewed that the body also needs to be renewed. The redeemed spirit needs a redeemed body—not a different body, but a renewed body. And that will be the spiritual body. Tertullian wrote, "And so the flesh shall rise again, wholly in each person, in its own identity, in its absolute integrity" (*On the Resurrection of the Flesh* 63). So yes, it will be the same body, reunited with the same spirit. But it will also have to be a changed body, ready to receive a changed (redeemed) spirit. As St. Paul said, "We shall all be changed" (1 Cor. 15:51).

The Legend of the Phoenix

St. Paul tells us that "the last enemy to be destroyed is death" (1 Cor. 15:26; cf. Rev. 21:4). To be honest, the Church Fathers were not all in agreement on whether the first humans were created immortal or were created mortal but with the *potential* to become immortal. St. Augustine thought that Adam and Eve were created mortal, but if they had not sinned, they would have gained immortality by eating from the tree of life (*Sermon* 155). But whether the Church Fathers and Mothers believed that, in the Fall, humans lost immortality or only the ability to gain it, they all would agree that immortality was the goal, and death was meant to be overcome. Death is not God's desire for humanity, and we could go so far as to say that it is a state that is not natural to humanity as we were originally created.

Writing about the separation of the spirit from the body, St. Augustine said this: "For the very violence with which body and soul are wrenched asunder, which in the living had been conjoined and closely intertwined, brings with it a harsh experience, jarring horridly on nature so long as it continues, till there comes a total loss of sensation, which arose from the very interpenetration of spirit and flesh" (*City of God* 13.6). In other words, when a person dies, he or she is in a state that is an existence in tension: it is not, in fact, resting in peace, but it is a time of waiting for the resolution of resurrection. It is sin (which itself is not natural to humanity) that causes death, along with everything that goes with it, including corruption and decay. Even though our spirits live on after our death, they live in the tension of waiting for the resurrection, when the body, too, is made immortal.

So, we have to be clear: resurrection is not simply "going to Heaven" and it does not happen at the time of physical death (Ratzinger, *Eschatology*, p. 160). Our spirits will be separated from our bodies for a time, and so, for a while, we do experience something of a disembodied existence — but again, this is not our natural state, and it is not our goal. Both Tertullian and Macrina taught that it is this time of separation that purifies both spirit and body and completes the process of our sanctification (sometimes called *theosis*, or "deification"). The body is purified in the earth, while the spirit is purified in Purgatory (I'll say more about Purgatory below), so that when they come back together in the resurrection, they are both ready for the Kingdom of Heaven (see Tertullian, *A Treatise on the Soul* 53).

A very interesting but little-known fact about the early Church is that for the first few centuries, the Church Fathers' favorite symbol of the resurrection was not an empty cross or even an empty tomb. It was the mythical bird known as the phoenix. St. Clement of Rome (bishop from 88 to 97) spent a lot of time talking about the phoenix in his letter to the Corinthian Christians (known as *1 Clement*). Tertullian mentions it (*On the Resurrection of the Flesh* 13), and St. Ambrose refers to it (*On Belief in the Resurrection* 59). Some of the Church Fathers seem to have believed it was a real bird, not just a myth, and they use it as part of their argument for the doctrine of resurrection, as if to say, if a bird can raise itself from the ashes of its own cremation fire, certainly God can raise people from the grave.

The myth of the phoenix is a story about a unique, exotic bird. In fact, there is only one in the world; she doesn't even have a mate. She lives for five hundred years, and at the end of her life cycle, she flies to her home in the East and makes a nest in a palm tree. The nest bursts into flames and becomes her funeral fire, but she emerges anew from the ashes to start the cycle again. It may seem strange to us that the early Christians would use such a legend as a symbol for the thing they believed was most true in the world—the Christ event. St. Ambrose even pointed out that the last time the bird was seen rising from the ashes was in the same year that Christ rose from His tomb. The phoenix, however, is not a metaphor for Christ per se, but for resurrection—not only Jesus' Resurrection, but our hope of resurrection as well. In churches in Rome, the image of the phoenix can still be found in mosaics from as late as the Middle Ages (for more on the phoenix, with some photos, see my books *A Week in the Life of Rome* and *Rome: A Pilgrim's Guide to the Eternal City*).

You might ask: Why didn't they prefer the symbol of the butterfly? It seems like the image of a caterpillar becoming a butterfly would make a better analogy for resurrection (not to mention the fact that the butterfly is real). But ancient people already thought of the butterfly as a symbol of the *soul* rising away from the body, so that didn't work for the resurrection of the flesh. The butterfly, to the ancient mind, was too light to represent a body. But a phoenix had flesh—in fact the legends specifically mention the phoenix's flesh. And it was the resurrection of the body that the Church Fathers wanted to emphasize. The phoenix didn't just rise to live again; she rose with incorruptible flesh. And this is exactly the point. When we rise again in the resurrection, we will not just be perfected versions of ourselves; we will also be perfected in the image of God—that is, we will be like Christ.

St. Macrina told her brother Gregory:

> Just as it is neither entirely the same thing as that seed nor something altogether different, so (she insisted) by these miracles performed on seeds you may now interpret the mystery of the resurrection. The divine power in the superabundance of omnipotence, does not only restore you

that body once dissolved, but makes great and splendid additions to it, whereby the human being is furnished in a manner still more magnificent ... and yet the human being does not lose itself.

So the resurrection is not only a restoration of the body, but our bodies will be brought to a complete perfection they never had in life. They will be glorified, as Jesus' divine nature glorified His body. They will be incorruptible (unable to die) and impassible (unable to suffer), but they will also be immutable—they will be unchanging—because change is a function of time, and the resurrection body must be suited to life in eternity, outside of the limits of time.

St. Irenaeus of Lyons (bishop from 177 to 202) wrote of what would come to be called the "wonderful exchange." He said, "The Word of God, our Lord Jesus Christ, who did, through his transcendent love, become what we are, that he might bring us to be even what he is himself" (*Against Heresies*, preface to bk. 5). In other words, Christ became what we are (human) so that we could become what He is (the perfect image of God). The biblical foundation of this concept can be seen in Isaiah 53:4–6 and Galatians 3:13–14. This is also what St. Peter meant when he said that we would come to be "partakers of the divine nature" (2 Pet. 1:4). Theologians sometimes refer to this as *theosis*, or "deification," though it does not mean we become gods; it means we become completely like God in the ways we were meant to be when we were created in His image.

So, the resurrection is both a return to the purity of humanity's innocence and the fulfillment of humanity's original purpose. It is going to back to where we started, but also going beyond where we started. We are both restored and transformed. The phoenix rises incorruptible. This is another paradox of the mystery of the resurrection: we are returned to a corporeal (bodily) existence, but it is also a new existence suited to the new realm of the Kingdom of Heaven. This is a return to wholeness yet without the struggle between the spirit and the flesh that often characterizes our earthly life when the body doesn't want to obey the will. As Pope St. John Paul II says in his *Theology of the Body*, as a person matures spiritually in this life, progressing in sanctification, the body learns to submit more and more to the spirit, and thus it becomes closer and closer to the way it will be in the resurrection life. And when our bodies are finally raised, that process of sanctification is completed and fulfilled. What is now the result of discipline will then be our natural state.

But we must not assume that this natural state is achieved by somehow transcending the body, much less discarding the body. When Jesus said that people will not get married in Heaven, He was making a statement not about the human body but rather about the need for procreation in this life that will not exist in the Kingdom. But make no mistake—life in the Kingdom is life in a body. Just as the body is now the spirit's interface with creation—and just as now we experience the beauty of creation through the senses of the body—so it will be in the spiritual realm. Eternal life may be outside of time, but it is not outside of creation (because the only existence outside of creation is the Creator, the Trinity). Just as you must not imagine the Kingdom as an intangible existence, you must also not imagine the Kingdom as only a mental existence. It is the case that truth is experienced through the mind (spirit), but truth without beauty would be an incomplete experience of creation. The reality is that beauty and truth are two sides of the same coin. They are both the self-expression of God in creation, and in order to experience

God truly, we will need to appreciate creation fully — and that will require a body.

If we're not entirely comfortable with a mythical bird as our symbol of resurrection, I would suggest we think of the Eucharist. The Body and Blood of Jesus in the Eucharist are the same body and blood that were born of Mary's womb, walked the earth, hung on a Cross, rose from the dead, and ascended into Heaven. And yet this Body and Blood are changed in a way that it is not accessible to the earthly senses the way the aspects (accidents) of bread and wine are (for more on the theology of the Eucharist, see my book *Handed Down: The Catholic Faith of the Early Christians*). All speculation of scars, age, and genitals aside — and even acknowledging that we will always interact with creation through a body — what we experience now in the Eucharistic elements is real and true, and yet it is a mystery that we could never have anticipated if it were not revealed to us. What we eat and drink is the Real Presence of the Body and Blood of the Lord — not in a crudely literal way, or in a spiritualized metaphorical way, but in a mystical way such that the elements are the *same* Body and Blood of the Lord as His historical physical flesh, but they are not *identical* to the flesh of Jesus. This is like our resurrection bodies: the same body, yet not identical to what it is now.

Having said that, in our time there is nothing wrong with using the image of the butterfly as a symbol for the resurrection. Our earthly bodies are like caterpillars — stuck on the ground, with limited visibility of the universe around us. But our resurrection bodies will be like those of butterflies. The same body that goes into the grave (chrysalis) will emerge. It will be the body of the same individual, but it will be suited to a new, heavenly reality, as the body of a butterfly is suited to flight. But as long as the caterpillar is a caterpillar, it could never truly imagine what it will be like to be a butterfly.

What About the In-Between Time?

The resurrection that we believe in does not happen at the time of our death. It is not as though each person is resurrected at (or shortly after) the time of his or her physical death. If that were the case, billions of people would be living the resurrection life in their spiritual bodies even now. But the resurrection is not an individual event. It is what is sometimes referred to as the "general resurrection," meaning that everyone will be raised at the same time. The resurrection, and the reconstitution of our bodies into spiritual bodies to be reunited with our spirits, will take place at the time of the second coming of Christ, which is the end of human history. Notice that in the parable, the ten bridesmaids were waiting for the groom. And the analogy for us is that we live in the age of the Church, when the Church (the Bride of Christ) waits for her Groom to return. When He does return, it will be time for the wedding (we'll talk about the parable of the wedding banquet a little later).

This life of the resurrection after the end of time and the second coming of Christ is what the book of Revelation refers to as the "New Jerusalem." It is also what Thomas Aquinas called the "Beatific Vision," in which the human person "sees" the divine essence directly and comes to immutable happiness and the full potential of understanding and knowing God as fully as he or she is known by God (1 Cor. 13:12). This is part of the reason there is no marriage in Heaven, because in Heaven there is a new primary union of the believer (as part of the Church, the Body of Christ and Bride of Christ) with the Trinity through

Jesus—the Body united with its Head, the Bride united with her Groom.

The resurrection cannot have taken place already for anyone but Jesus (and Mary—more on her below), because everyone else who has died has left his or her body behind, and the elements of those bodies are still part of the earth. For the saints, these are their relics, which we venerate at holy sites and which are placed in our altars when the altars are consecrated (see Rev. 6:9–11). And the ongoing connection of those relics with the spirit of the saint who owns them and who is in the presence of the risen Christ means that we can come close to Christ by coming close to the relics. Eventually, though, this world will come to an end, and then those relics, along with the remains of everyone else who ever lived, will be raised. Gregory of Nyssa (through his sister Macrina) taught that there *must* be an end to human history (and an end to human procreation and the creation of new souls), because for the resurrection to take place, all of the elements of the earth that once were part of human bodies would have to be brought up into the resurrection bodies of so many people.

So, what happens in the meantime? A person who dies now (not to mention many years ago) will have to wait for the resurrection in that state of tension when the spirit waits to be reunited with the body. People in this state are dead and have not yet been raised to life. But does that mean they are unconscious? What do they experience in this time of "chrysalis," between the existence of caterpillar and butterfly?

It should be pointed out that the parable of the rich man and Lazarus takes place in this in-between time. Both of these men have died, but the resurrection has not yet taken place. They are conscious of their situation, and they remember their loved ones. Of course, we can't push this parable too far or take it too literally as a picture of the afterlife, especially since Jesus told it before His own Resurrection. Macrina reminds us that reading literal eyes that look up to Heaven or a literal tongue that is thirsty is to misinterpret the passage, because the bodies of the rich man and of Lazarus are still in their graves. But we can deduce from Jesus' parable that people who have died do not simply "sleep" until the resurrection or exist in some unconscious state of suspended animation until they "wake up" at the end of time. This is important, because we believe in the communion of the saints, and we believe that the spirits of the saints can hear our prayers and pray for us even now. (For more on this, and for an explanation of why the ability to hear prayer is not an attribution of divinity to dead people—that is, a form of idolatry—see my book *Handed Down: The Catholic Faith of the Early Christians*.) To speak of someone who has passed on as "asleep" (such as in 1 Cor. 11:30 or 1 Thess. 4:14–15) is simply a euphemism for death and does not imply that the person is unconscious or unaware.

Even the concept of "resting in peace" is a euphemism that applies more to the body than to the spirit, because, as Tertullian pointed out, some people go to Hell immediately after death, and they do not need to wait for a resurrection body to be punished (like the rich man in the parable; see Tertullian, *A Treatise on the Soul* 43, 53, and *On the Resurrection of the Flesh* 17). To say very much about Hell would require another book, so it's not my intention here to explain the concept of Hell or what happens to people who do not finally receive salvation. For our purposes, it is enough to say that Tertullian seems to have believed those people consigned to Hell would be in something of a "dreamlike" existence, rather like what many people in the Roman world believed that the afterlife would be for everyone. But since Tertullian saw the human spirit as the part of us primarily to blame for sin, even the spirit in Hell must be aware enough to experience the regret of not making it into Heaven. For Gregory of Nyssa, this is, in fact, the primary "torture" of Hell: regret. Regret and shame. Macrina said, "Remorse ... is a whip."

We should also assume that while there are no desires that come from lack or want in the Kingdom of Heaven, that does not apply to Hell. The fact that Hell is a punishment assumes that those who end up there must be aware of their loss, especially the loss of peace. Hell is not so much a "place" of torment (since God is omnipresent and there is no place outside of His influence), but rather it is to be thought of as a *situation* in which a person is cut off from God. The person who rejects any connection to God in the present life is granted that same wish in the afterlife, but the difference is that in Hell the person's mind is eternally occupied with looking back on life and mourning the very attachment to earthly life that caused the separation from God. This is the "outer darkness" of Jesus' parable of the wedding banquet (Matt. 22:13), where there is weeping (remorse) and gnashing of teeth (regret).

There is some disagreement among the Church Fathers as to whether punishment in Hell is literal—that is, "physical"—and therefore requires a body. For some of them, this becomes part of their argument for the resurrection body—people must be raised bodily so the damned can be tortured. In any case, in this intermediate phase before the resurrection, there is no body to be punished, even for those in Hell. After the resurrection, it may be the case that those who are judged and condemned will receive their spiritual body to be punished in it; nevertheless, the later Church Fathers seem to have believed that even then the torture of Hell would be primarily spiritual or intellectual, rather than physical.

So, when a person dies, his or her spirit leaves the earthly realm, which is bound by time, and, we might say, enters eternity. But the body remains in the world of time and three-dimensional space. Spirit and body are separated from the moment of death until the resurrection, which will take place at the end of time (Ratzinger, *Eschatology*, p. 252). But although they are separated in the interim, each spirit is eternally and inseparably connected to the same body it had in life, in spite of decay. According to Gregory and Macrina, the spirit is the guardian of the elements of the body, watching over each particle so that nothing is lost. All of this means that none of our loved ones who have passed on have experienced the resurrection yet. They all exist in this intermediate state. They are conscious and aware. There is an initial judgment to determine who will go directly to Hell (Rev. 20:12–13). But those who die in Christ are alive in Christ, and by virtue of their union with Christ, they can hear our prayers when we pray to them. They remember us, and they can pray for us. But they are temporarily separated from their bodies.

Therefore, whatever the dead are experiencing now, it is not the resurrection, and it is not the New Jerusalem of the book of Revelation. This interim is to be distinguished from the fully realized Kingdom of Heaven, which has not yet been revealed, even to the dead. What the dead experience now has been called Paradise, or resting in peace, or Abraham's Bosom, as in the parable (see Ratzinger, *Eschatology*, pp. 219, 246). According to St. Augustine, Paradise and the Kingdom of Heaven are different things (*On the Soul and Its Origin* 1.10; *City of God* 13.20–21). The term "paradise" is, of course, a reference to the original state of humanity in the Garden of Eden, but the Paradise of the afterlife is not simply a return to the past. It is a return to the peace and joy of innocence, but it is also a moving forward toward the ultimate goal of humanity, which is redemption and union with God. So Paradise is possible now, but the Kingdom comes later.

What about Purgatory?

Before we can say anything definitive about Purgatory, we have to acknowledge that, just as a whole book could be written about Hell, a whole book could be written about Purgatory (for my take on it, see the section on Purgatory in my book *Handed Down: The Catholic Faith of the Early Christians*). Having said that, the Church is reluctant to clarify a doctrine of Purgatory in much detail because both historically and ecumenically, there is a wide variety of beliefs about Purgatory that are not all mutually exclusive. In other words, we must leave room for a range of ways of understanding Purgatory. Especially when it comes to dialogue with the Eastern Orthodox traditions, there is a general admission that the concept is clouded in mystery, and in many ways it is simply not accessible to our experience or our understanding.

The Church Fathers, of course, did believe in Purgatory, and they did believe that some kind of reparation for sin would be made after death. But Tertullian, for example, placed Purgatory in Hades and spoke of it as though it was simply a temporary version of Hell. He warned his readers, "Lest this judge [God] deliver you over to the angel who is to execute the sentence, and he commit you to the prison of hell, out of which there will be no dismissal until the smallest even of your delinquencies be paid off in the period before the resurrection ..." (*A Treatise on the Soul* 35). He also said, "Every soul is detained in safe keeping in Hades until the day of the Lord" (*A Treatise on the Soul* 55). When he says "every soul," he means everyone except the martyrs. He believed that the martyrs never had to go to Purgatory, but that everyone else would spend the whole of the intermediate time in Purgatory. So Tertullian seems to think no one leaves Purgatory until the resurrection, and currently the only people in Paradise are the martyrs and other saints.

But other Church Fathers, and most of the later ones, believed that Purgatory was not something that lasted the whole of the interim, and that those who did not go directly to Paradise at their deaths (probably everyone besides Mary and the martyrs) would eventually leave Purgatory and enter Paradise. For most of us, when we die, we can expect to go to Purgatory, and then after that enter into Paradise, where we will wait out the rest of the intermediate time until the resurrection.

Although we might say that people "go to" Purgatory, however, this is not a physical place any more than Hell is. The best way to understand Purgatory is that it is a purification that prepares us to enter Paradise, where we will be in the presence of God. Just as, in the Old Testament, something that made a person "unclean" would have to be purified before that person could worship God at the Temple, so our sin makes us "unclean" before God, and we must be purified before we can enter into His presence. The word "Purgatory" means "purification." As Pope Benedict XVI pointed out, entering the Kingdom of Heaven requires that we are first purified of whatever is not essential to our personhood, whatever we carry with us from our earthly life that is not part of us, especially the impurities of sin and the remnants of our guilt (Ratzinger, *Eschatology*, p. 235). As St. Paul said, "He who began a good work in you will bring it to completion at the day of Jesus Christ" (Phil. 1:6).

What *Really* Happens after We Die

Gregory of Nyssa called Purgatory a "second death" that would "cleanse [us] from the remnants" of our attachments to this life. If we die with attachments to the world, it is Purgatory that will burn them away, replacing the desires of looking back with the joy of looking forward to eternal life (see 1 Cor. 3:15). The image of fire is not to be taken literally, because after all, the person in Purgatory has no body. The image of fire is an analogy of the crucible, the way gold or silver is purified by putting it over the fire (see Ps. 66:10; Prov. 17:3).

Macrina used another analogy for Purgatory. Rather than speaking of it as a purifying fire, she said to imagine a rope encrusted with clay. If you wanted to pull the rope through a hole that was just big enough for the rope itself, you would have to pull quite violently to scrape off the clay as the rope went through the hole. If the rope could feel pain, it would not be a pleasant process, but when the rope emerged on the other side of the hole, it would be cleaned of the clay. Macrina's point is that Purgatory is not so much a punishment as a cleaning. The dirtier one is, the more the cleaning will hurt, but God does it out of love, not as a punishment.

Macrina also said that we all die with different amounts of clay on us, different amounts of impurities. And the more dirt there is on the rope, or the more impurities there are in the precious metal, the more time it will take to "burn" it off, and so Purgatory comes to be associated with time. We have to acknowledge that Purgatory exists in the realm outside of linear time, however, so to speak of spending an amount of time in Purgatory could be as much of a misunderstanding as it would be to assume that Purgatory entails literal fire. The idea that one would spend a certain amount of time in Purgatory for particular sins, and indeed the idea that indulgences would shave off specific amounts of time from Purgatory, are medieval ideas influenced by the development of a credit economy in Europe. But these concepts were not in the minds of the Church Fathers and Mothers. Incidentally, Macrina taught that Jesus' parables that seem to imply different rewards in the afterlife (such as the parable of the talents; Matt. 25:14–30) are really about Purgatory, not about the Kingdom of Heaven. She also said that Jesus' references to judgment as being "thrown into the fire" are also really about Purgatory. Whether we choose to agree with her interpretation of those Gospel passages, it is clear that Purgatory is a reality that is part of the intermediate time before the resurrection, and it is not something that anyone will experience with their resurrection body. Also, Purgatory is not Hell. It is only for those who will eventually go on to salvation, so no one goes from Purgatory into Hell, only from Purgatory into Paradise.

St. Augustine wrote:

Temporary punishments are suffered by some in this life only, by others after death, by others both now and then; but all of them before the last and strictest judgment. But of those who suffer temporary punishments after death, all are not doomed to those everlasting pains that are to follow that judgment; for to some, as we have already said, what is not remitted in this world is remitted in the next; that is, they are not punished with the eternal punishment of the world to come (*City of God* 21.13)

There is another aspect of all of this to consider. Just as the human spirit remains connected to its body during the time of separation, human actions have repercussions that continue on in the world even after the person has died. So, we need Purgatory not only to cleanse us of the remainder of our sinful impurities but also to purify us of the negative consequences of our actions that outlive us. If we have made others suffer, and if that suffering goes on after we are dead, we cannot be completely redeemed until that suffering is ended. Pope Benedict XVI said that one cannot expect to receive the reward of eternal life while the consequences of mistakes made in life still effect the world. Purgatory is the purging of "unresolved guilt" (Ratzinger, *Eschatology*, p. 189). This is another reason why human history cannot go on forever. At some point, all suffering must be ended in order for there to be full joy in the Kingdom of Heaven (Ratzinger, *Eschatology*, p. 188).

Although we should not go too far in assuming that Purgatory is a time-bound sentence, perhaps it is the case that a person is not released from Purgatory into Paradise until the negative effects of his or her actions have disappeared from the world. Pope Benedict XVI wrote that Purgatory is neither temporal nor eternal, but a transition between the two. It cannot be measured by time, but that does not mean it is instantaneous (Ratzinger, *Eschatology*, p. 230). It is a process of God's grace, motivated by His love, which prepares us for entering into the presence of God and the saints—first in Paradise, then in the Kingdom of Heaven (Ratzinger, *Eschatology*, pp. 230–231, and see his summary of what we know about Purgatory on pp. 223–224).

Death Is Like Another Birth

I admit I don't know anything about the afterlife firsthand. But we have the inspired writings of the apostles in the New Testament, and after that, the writings of the Church Fathers and Mothers—people who were very wise, very spiritual, and very close to God. We cannot know for sure what the afterlife is like, and yet a big part of our Faith is the confidence that death is not the end of existence. The best anyone can do is to read the Scriptures and the writings of those whose interpretations of Scripture have become the Tradition of the Church, and then put that together with personal experience of God in life, and decide what to believe.

I believe that death is like another birth. You know, from the moment you were created—from the moment you were given life—you existed in a womb. That nine months in the womb seemed to you like a lifetime, and it was warm, and you had everything you needed, and it was comfortable. But eventually, you came to experience suffering. There was pain, and there was struggle, and maybe there was even fear. And when the day came, you were traumatically ripped from the only world you knew—a world you liked, by the way—and you were born into a new world of bright lights and loud noises.

Death is like that. It's like being taken from the only world you know and being born into a new existence that you could not have imagined. But for those of us who mourn the deaths of loved ones, it's like being a younger twin. Imagine that for your whole existence, not only have you lived in a warm, comfortable place, but you've had a companion—someone who is so close to you that it's like they're part of you. And then that day comes, and this person is taken from you and born into a new life. Now, we know that there's only a minute or two after the birth of the first twin before the younger one is born. But in that minute or two, in the mind of the younger twin, the loved one is gone.

Anyone who mourns a loved one is like that younger twin, living in that minute or two after the birth of his or her loved one into a new life, but before the younger twin's own birth into that new life. When the younger twin is finally born, the twins are reunited. And although, in our lives, that "minute or two" might last years, I believe — to put it bluntly — that Heaven is a reunion. And in the light of eternity, the years we spent apart will seem like a minute or two. And just like someone who has been alive only nine months cannot possibly imagine what life after birth will be like, and how long it can last, in the same way, someone who has been alive for only a few decades cannot possibly imagine what eternity is like.

So, in those moments when it's impossible to imagine what the next life is like, remember that the baby in the womb could not imagine the joys of this life. Or, to use another metaphor, the caterpillar cannot imagine what it's like to be a butterfly. And if you're ever tempted to think that maybe there is no God, because you think, "What kind of God would allow someone to suffer, or take my loved one from me?" remember the answer: the same God who turns a caterpillar into a butterfly.

6

Heaven Is a Reunion

Alexandra shushed her husband and gave him a stern, wide-eyed look as she put her finger to her lips. "Do you want him to hear you?" she whispered.

Bill lowered his voice. "We should have named him Bruce, or Chuck. Then, when people heard his name, they would think of someone cool like Bruce Willis or Chuck Norris. Why did you have to insist on naming him Ulysses?"

Alexandra was indignant. "Don't blame me that he's the awkward kid in his class."

"This is bad." Bill tried to divert the conversation in another direction. "It was fine when he was a little kid and we could just have relatives at his parties. But now he's at the age when it's important to be cool, and he cares what the other kids think. He won't be happy with a family party. He wants a party with friends, but the kid doesn't have any friends."

"We'll just invite his whole class," Alexandra whispered in frustration. "What else can we do?" And that's what they did. As Ulysses's birthday approached, his parents sent him to school with enough party invitations for his whole class. When he handed them out, the kids with manners made excuses about being busy that day. But most of the kids made fun of Ulysses, mocking him, and telling him they wouldn't be caught dead at his lame party.

As he cried himself to sleep that night, his parents brainstormed in whispers once again. After about thirty minutes of tense complaining and scapegoating, Alexandra had an idea. "The church. We invite all the kids from the church who are about his age. They don't go to his school, but he knows them well enough so the party won't be full of strangers." Bill nodded, relieved to have a solution.

Bill and Alexandra spoke with the children's director at the church, who used the e-mail list to send out the invitations. And the plan worked, because on the day of Ulysses's party, the Pizza Arcade was packed with kids, all screaming with joy. Bill rubbed his temples. But as he looked over to see if his son was having a good time, he saw a bigger boy shove Ulysses. He ran over and helped Ulysses up. "What's going on?"

With tears in his eyes, Ulysses sobbed out the words, "He's always mean to me." It turned out that the only kid from Ulysses' class who did show up was the school bully. He was the reason the other kids picked on Ulysses. So Bill found out the bigger kid's name and called his parents to come and pick him up and take him home. Then he called the principal and told her everything. Eventually the bully was expelled from the school, and the other kids who had made Ulysses's life miserable were reprimanded.

After the party, it was clear that Ulysses had forgotten all about the bully. The kids from church had brought gifts, even though they didn't know Ulysses very well. The party was a huge success, and all the kids who were there talked about it until it reached legendary status. In fact, a couple of years later, when Ulysses went to the middle school, a bunch of kids there recognized his name as the one who had that famous party. Between that and his new friends from church, he had plenty of friends at school, and none of them thought he was awkward.

* * *

Do you remember what it was like to be so young that a thing like a party seemed like your whole world? When you're too small to reach things on high shelves, and you can't drive a car or have your own money, then the things you look forward to, such as pizza and arcade parties, take on a bigger-than-life importance. And any setback, especially one that makes you less popular, seems like the end of the world. When we become adults, we gain a bigger perspective. We might still get invited to parties, but we also have responsibilities and other things to look forward to that allow us to see past the party. But still there is always that temptation to be too shortsighted. If we're busy or stressed, it's tempting just to live for the weekend and not think too much past making plans for Friday night or Saturday. Or even if we're more responsible than that, we can get caught up in goals and plans for the near future and forget to think about the long term. In other words, we often make the same mistake that kids make — maybe on a bigger scale, but we are still not thinking of the big picture. And by "big picture" I mean eternity.

When Jesus told the parable of the wedding banquet (Matt. 22:1–14), He was criticizing people who were being too shortsighted. They were more worried about their farms or their businesses than the eternal destiny of their souls. These were serious grown-ups who took seriously everything except their relationship with God.

What *Really* Happens after We Die

Heaven Is a Party

Jesus began this parable by saying, "The Kingdom of Heaven may be compared to a king who gave a marriage feast for his son." So the first thing we see is that this is another one of those "the Kingdom is like this" parables. And what does Jesus say that it will be like? A wedding reception. Remember that the parable of the ten bridesmaids was about waiting for the groom. Jesus Christ is the Groom, and the Church is His Bride. In the age of the Church, we are waiting for the return of the Groom. It's as though Jesus' first advent was His engagement to the Church, and His second coming will be when He arrives for the wedding itself (for more on the second coming of Christ and the end of history as the wedding of Christ and His Bride, the Church, see my book *The Wedding of the Lamb: A Historical Approach to the Book of Revelation*).

But just like any wedding reception, when the invitations go out, everyone is expected to RSVP; that is, you have to reply to the invitation and let the couple know whether you are planning to attend—whether you accept the invitation. With the heavenly wedding, the invitation went out to all of humanity when Jesus died on the Cross for us. You may be familiar with crucifixes that show the sign above Jesus' head. It has the letters "INRI" (for the Latin words *Iesus Nazarenus, Rex Iudaeorum*: "Jesus of Nazareth, King of the Jews"). But I like to say that the sign on the Cross might as well have had the letters "RSVP," because the Cross is an invitation that demands a response from us, if we want it to be effective for us (for more on this, see my book *Spiritual Blueprint: How We Live, Work, Love, Play, and Pray*). If we do not respond to the Cross with a commitment to Christ in the sacraments of the Church, and a life lived in gratitude and service to God and neighbor, then we have effectively responded to the invitation with an RSVP of no. And those who do not respond positively to the invitation should not be surprised when they do not end up at the party. Jesus said Heaven is a party, but if you want to be at the party, you have to RSVP with a yes to Jesus.

There are a lot of theories about the man in the parable who comes to the wedding without the proper wedding garment. Many people speculate that the wedding garment is a metaphor for a person's lifestyle. In other words, a person may respond with a yes to Jesus' invitation, but if that person lives selfishly, he or she has not really "put on the Lord Jesus Christ" (Rom. 13:14), and therefore, Jesus will say to this person, "I never knew you" (Matt. 7:21-23). Regardless of how we interpret the details of this parable, we must notice that when Jesus gets to the end of it, He shifts from speaking in an allegory to speaking quite literally. All of a sudden, one guy who was at the wedding is thrown out—not into the street or even into prison, but "into the outer darkness; there men will weep and gnash their teeth."

The end result of rejecting Jesus' invitation to the forgiveness of the Cross is something that should be obvious: the person who rejects forgiveness does not get forgiveness. The person who chooses not to have a relationship with God in Christ in the present life will have that choice honored in the next life, and will be separated from God for eternity. Although we don't know what it means to be "outside" of the presence of an omnipresent God, it is clear that not everyone will be in the Kingdom of Heaven. Although it would be more comfortable to believe that everyone will eventually receive salvation (a theory called "universalism"), it is clear that Jesus did not believe this. Jesus believed that there will be those who are at the eternal party, and those who are not. We should not be so shortsighted as to take the invitation lightly.

What *Really* Happens after We Die

If we believe what Jesus said, that the Kingdom of Heaven will be like a banquet, doesn't that imply that we will be eating and drinking there? In fact, Jesus also promised His disciples that the next time He drank wine, He would be drinking it with them in the Kingdom (Matt. 26:29; Mark 14:25). But on the other hand, we remember that St. Paul wrote, "Food is for the stomach and the stomach for food, and God will destroy both one and the other" (1 Cor. 6:13; see also Col. 2:20–22). Is this a contradiction between Jesus and Paul? Does Paul think our resurrection bodies will not have stomachs? Some of the Church Fathers (and Mothers, including Macrina) believed that people will not eat in Heaven. Others, including St. Augustine, believed that eating will be optional. Augustine said that Jesus ate after His Resurrection to prove that He was not a ghost, but He would not have *needed* to eat to live (*City of God* 22.19). Since hunger and thirst are not part of the spiritual body, any eating done in the heavenly realm will be done for other reasons.

It seems reasonable to assume that just as St. Paul often speaks of "the flesh" when he really means the sinful *desires* of the flesh, here he speaks of "the stomach" when he really means the *desires* of the stomach (and other body parts) that will not exist in the heavenly realm. In fact, we are compelled to take this interpretation of the Pauline passages when we look at what Jesus said and what was revealed to John in the book of Revelation. In addition to the fact that Jesus ate after His Resurrection (Luke 24:42–43; see John 21:12–13), He also told His disciples that many people from east and west will come to the banquet table in the Kingdom, and there they will eat bread. He said, "Blessed is he who shall eat bread in the Kingdom of God" (see Luke 14:15; Matt. 8:11).

It is true that on some level, this may be a reference to the Eucharistic bread, Christ's Body and Blood. Jesus may be pronouncing a blessing on everyone whose participation in the Eucharist on earth will bring them to the heavenly banquet, because the Eucharist is the foretaste of the wedding feast of the Lamb. And in fact, in the book of Revelation, the angel tells John to write this: "Blessed are those who are invited to the marriage supper of the Lamb" (Rev. 19:9). We hear this line spoken by the priest at Mass, connecting the Holy Eucharist in the Mass to the wedding banquet of the Kingdom of Heaven. But still, if it is indeed a wedding *supper*, then doesn't that imply that the experience of Heaven includes eating and drinking?

What is more important than the actual eating and drinking, though, is the table fellowship with our brothers and sisters and the intimate fellowship with Christ that is granted to us at the Eucharistic table. Both of these will be perfected and brought to fullness in the Kingdom of Heaven. We will experience fellowship with the saints, and the Beatific Vision, joys that will far surpass the joys we get from eating and drinking with friends. Jesus is using the joy of a banquet celebration to help us understand the joy of the communion of Heaven—but it's one of those cases in which He is saying, "If it's this good in the present life, just imagine how much better it will be in eternity."

So, whatever joys we now get from eating and drinking, that kind of joy will exist in the fellowship that we will have with loved ones, with the saints, and with Jesus. We will not *need* to eat or drink, and if there is no chewing, swallowing, and digesting, we will not miss it. We do believe that our spiritual bodies will have senses that will allow us to continue to interface with creation, but we don't know what that means for the senses of taste and smell that make eating and drinking enjoyable. It could be that, just as the caterpillar cannot fathom the difference between legs and wings, we cannot fathom the way in which our senses will be glorified, and therefore heightened. Does this mean that I will finally get my wish: that I can eat anything I want and not gain weight? Could it be that Heaven has food, but it doesn't have calories? Maybe that's one way to think of it, but the important thing is that the joys we get from eating and drinking now are nothing compared with the glorified joys of communion with the saints and union with the Divine.

Heaven Is Our Hope

Let's be clear about something: Heaven will not be boring. In the early Church, it seems that some philosophers argued against the Christian doctrine of the resurrection body by saying that if the earthly functions of the body will not be necessary, then the body is useless. Tertullian responded by assuring them that we will not be idle in the afterlife. There will be things to do (*On the Resurrection of the Flesh* 60). Primarily, our full-time job in eternity will be to worship God. Notice that in John's vision of Heaven, worship is continuous (Rev. 4:8–5:14). And just as we do on earth, in the Kingdom we will not worship God with our minds only, but also with our bodies.

But in addition to the worship of God, there is fellowship with other people. In other words, we will be able to interact with others, from asking St. Peter a theological question, to apologizing to the awkward kid from our fourth-grade class. Do you want to have breakfast with St. John? Coffee with St. James (first figure out which James you're thinking of)? Beer with Martin Luther? Yeah, he'll probably be there, the old curmudgeon. A glass of wine with Pope St. John Paul II? Tea with Mary? Why not! Okay, I don't know for sure about the beverages, but the conversation—just think of the conversation!

The Kingdom of Heaven is not just Jesus and I staring into each other's eyes for all eternity, as if there were no one else there. The Beatific Vision does not put blinders on you so that you can see *only* God (because you can't really love God unless you love others too [1 John 4:7–21]). It is also not the absorption of my personality into the universe, or into some universal being. I will retain my individuality and personality, and so will you. But I will also become a communal being in a way that was never possible before, due to original sin and the selfish tendencies that come with it. Remember that, as St. Augustine said, all sin ultimately comes from fear (fear of loss, fear of not getting what we want, the fear of self-preservation). But there will be no fear in the Kingdom of Heaven, so for that reason (and other reasons) there will be no selfishness, and we will be able finally to be fully selfless — to love ourselves without our self-love ever diminishing the way we love God and neighbor.

The resurrection life is the life in which our fullest humanity is realized. As Pope Benedict XVI wrote (when he was Cardinal Ratzinger), to be accepted into eternal life is to be accepted into God's life — that is, the life of immortality and relationship. He said that "part of the Christian idea of immortality is fellowship with other human beings" and that Heaven will be a perfect union, not only with God, but with the communion of the saints. It is "the fulfillment of all human communion" (Ratzinger, *Eschatology*, pp. 158–159, 235). In fact, the future Holy Father pointed out that our very identity and personality — whatever is the essence of who we are as individuals — exists only as a function of being in relationship with others (*Eschatology*, pp. 183–184). So, just as the resurrection perfects the personal body, it also perfects the Body of Christ, the Church. Far from being just about me and Jesus, the Beatific Vision draws us inward to the life of the

Trinity and also radiates outward to include all those, from every time in human history, who have loved the Lord.

It is interesting that when Jesus used the analogy of the grain of wheat to talk about death and resurrection (John 12:24), He said that unless the grain of wheat dies and goes into the earth, *it remains alone*. We may think we have friends here and now, but when we come to the fellowship of the saints, the warmth of that fellowship and the pure desire we will have to be in selfless relationship with others will make our best friendships on earth seem like loneliness in comparison. For those who die in Christ, Heaven is not just a party — it's a reunion. And we will be reunited with all those we loved who passed on before and after us.

St. Ambrose wrote this in a eulogy for his brother:

> It is a pleasure to believe this, a joy to hope for it ... and so long as I live I will never allow myself to be cheated of this hope. For what comfort have I left but that I hope to come quickly to you, my brother, and that your departure will not cause a long severance between us, and that it may be granted me, through your intercessions, that you may quickly call me, who longs for you (*On Belief in the Resurrection* 134–135).

Our bodies are the interface with creation, and therefore they are the way we interact with other created beings. So, we will need our spiritual bodies to interact fully with others in the Kingdom, including to whatever extent we will eat and drink with them. This does not mean that we can't recognize and interact with loved ones before the resurrection — there are many accounts of people on their deathbeds seeing relatives who have passed on before them, presumably having come to be with them through the transition. But it does seem as though we will have to wait until the resurrection of our bodies to be able to hug them.

St. Jerome wrote these comforting words to a widow:

> Thus when we have to face the hard and cruel necessity of death, we are upheld by this consolation, that we shall shortly see again those whose absence we now mourn. For their end is not called death but a slumber and a falling asleep.... Victorious now and free from care he looks down upon you in your struggle, nay more, he prepares for you a place near to himself; for his love and affection toward you are still the same as when, disregarding his claim on you as a husband, he resolved to treat you even on earth as a sister. (Letter 75, *To Theodora*)

Therefore, although we grieve for our loved ones who have passed away, we grieve with hope (1 Thess. 4:13–18) and with patience (Ambrose, *On the Belief in the Resurrection* 11) — because Heaven is a reunion.

What We Know for Sure

It should go without saying that there is more we don't know about the afterlife than we do know. But in our exploration of Scripture and the Church Fathers, we are attempting to clarify what we can assume about our future existence in eternity, and specifically about the resurrection body. Although there has been a lot of speculation throughout history — some of it edifying, some of it perhaps less so — still there are some things we can say that all Christians should believe about Heaven. Here I will attempt to lay out succinctly what I believe we can know for sure.

What *Really* Happens after We Die

The ministry of Jesus Christ is bookended by two weddings: the Wedding at Cana, and the Wedding of the Lamb. It all began at the Wedding at Cana (John 2:1–11), where Jesus performed His first miracle: changing water into wine just so that the enjoyment of the party could go on. But, of course, that passage ends with John telling us that from this time on, "his disciples believed in him." At this wedding, Jesus seemed reluctant to begin His ministry, but through the intercession of Mary, He gave the world its first glimpse of His divinity. At Cana, Mary gave her Son to the world and He began His work of redemption—the Groom was betrothed to his Bride, which is His Mystical Body—all of us who would become His Church.

The first death

When any person comes to the end of this phase of life, his or her soul, or spirit, is separated from its body, and the body dies and begins to decay. The exception to this are those few saints who were so holy in life that their bodies do not show evidence of the effects of sin and remain incorrupt. They still die, and their spirits ascend to the heavenly realm, but their bodies do not decay. The fact that a saint's body remains incorrupt could be evidence that he or she did not have to experience the cleansing of Purgatory. We believe that martyrs do not go through Purgatory, because their ultimate sacrifice has purified them of all sin. We should also point out that Mary is the Queen of All Saints precisely because she was so perfectly without sin (she is *full of grace*, or as my Wesleyan friends would say, entirely sanctified) that after her death her body not only did not decay but was assumed into Heaven to be reunited with her spirit at that time. Other than Jesus, Mary is the only person who does not have to wait until the end of human history to experience the resurrection.

There will be an initial judgment at the time of an individual's death, since those who have rejected the forgiveness that Jesus Christ offers will know immediately that they are not to receive salvation, and they will suffer the consequences of a life that ignored their Creator. We may call this "going to Hell," but this is not the final judgment, nor is it the final punishment.

In any case, we know that we do not become angels, and although it is possible that some who are destined for eternal separation from God may hang around as ghosts for a while, those who die in Christ do not become ghosts.

Purgatory and Paradise

Between the time of an individual's death and the end of human history, that person's body remains on the earth. All but the incorrupt will experience decay — ashes to ashes, and dust to dust, as the body is reduced to its elements and seems to become part of the earth. Most people's spirits will go through a purification that we call Purgatory. Once the spirit is purified, it enters Paradise. As Jesus said to the "good thief" on the cross next to him, "Today you will be with me in Paradise" (Luke 23:43). Notice that for all His talk about the Kingdom, Jesus did not say, "Today you will be with me in the Kingdom." That will come later, at the end of history and the time of the resurrection.

So, our hope for the afterlife comes in two phases (Ratzinger, *Eschatology*, p. 247). The first phase is Paradise, and the second phase is the Kingdom of Heaven, though we may use the word "Heaven" as an umbrella term for the whole thing. Heaven, such as it is before the resurrection, is Paradise. But whatever Paradise is like, it will be experienced *without* the resurrection body. The spirit and the body remain connected, however, because even in Paradise, when the body is decaying on the earth, that body is still an essential part of the individual's personhood.

The Resurrection

There will come a time when the age of the Church, and then all of human history, will come to an end. This is often referred to as "the end of the world," but it is not the end of creation. Creation will not be destroyed; it will be renewed and redeemed. This is also referred to as the "second coming" of Christ (see, for example, 1 Thess. 4:15–17). Keeping in mind that directional language such as ascending and descending is probably metaphorical (Ratzinger, *Eschatology*, p. 237), we can at least say that this is the time when Jesus Christ will reveal Himself to the world in some very obvious way (see Matt. 24:26–28, 37–39; Luke 17:22–33), and after that it will be too late to change one's decisions. After this, all bodies will be raised and reunited with the same spirits that inhabited them in life. God will raise and reconstitute the very elements of the same bodies that lived, and yet these bodies will be transformed in a way that makes them suited for the spiritual realm. After this general resurrection, there will be a final judgment, and those spirits who were in Hell will now go (embodied) to their eternal separation from God. This is called the "second death" (Rev. 20:14; for more on this, see my book *The Wedding of the Lamb*).

Our resurrection bodies will retain the integrity of our individuality, including our maleness or femaleness, though we will have no sexual desire. Our spiritual bodies will be the same bodies we had in our earthly life but will be transformed and glorified. Lost body parts will be returned to us, and symmetry will be restored to perfect proportion. There will be no bodily suffering of any kind, and the bodily experience will be that of the prime of life. We may still have scars from our life's journey if those scars will be a source of joy or gratitude, but any injury that has caused pain will be perfectly healed. We will not experience hunger or thirst, though we may have the option of eating and drinking for the pure enjoyment of it. Our bodies will still be our interface with creation, but only in ways that result in joy.

The Kingdom of Heaven

Those spirits who were in Purgatory or Paradise will enter their final reward, the Kingdom of Heaven. Although there is an aspect of the Kingdom that is already made manifest by the first advent of Christ (Luke 17:21), it is not fully realized until the resurrection. In other words, the Kingdom may be within us now, but at the resurrection, we will be within the Kingdom (for more on the Kingdom of Heaven, see my book *The Wedding of the Lamb*). We will live in our resurrection bodies in the heavenly realm. This realm is also called the New Jerusalem.

We will be reunited with our loved ones and friends, we will know fellowship and conversation with the saints, and we will have perfect and direct knowledge of God. Imagine the feeling you get at a dinner party with your closest friends — the feeling of having set aside all work, deadlines, worries, and anxieties, and the only thing on your mind is the pure joy of good food and drink and being surrounded by people who love you. If you've had those fleeting moments of undiluted happiness, then imagine feeling like that for all eternity — imagine the relaxed confidence that this feeling will never go away.

The ministry of Jesus ends with the Wedding of the Lamb, when the engagement period (the age of the Church in human history) is over and the union between Christ and those who have accepted His invitation is consummated in perfection and in the fullest realization of human potential. Since God is love, and love is eternal (1 Cor. 13:13), eternity itself will be characterized by love (Ratzinger, *Eschatology*, pp. 259–260)—when we, in our whole personhood, spirit and body, have been perfected and glorified, and we can finally hug and be hugged—not only by the loved ones we mourned in life, but by Jesus, and His Mother, Mary.

7

Connecting with the Cloud

Maria followed her grandmother around everywhere she went. From the time she could walk, she hardly ever left her grandmother's side. So, whenever it was time for the ball game, Maria was there on the couch next to her grandma, eyes glued to the TV, watching the Cubs. And every spring, Maria's grandmother would buy her the rookie cards of all the new players in the league.

But Maria was impatient. After the first few games, she wanted to trade away most of the cards and keep only the cards of the players she thought were the best. She made quick judgments about the future of the players and wrote many off as destined to go back to the minors. But Grandma was wise. She didn't let Maria trade away those cards. She told Maria to be patient, because you never know who will have a great career. You don't know yet whose rookie cards are going to be valuable. It's too early to tell.

So, Maria reluctantly saved all the rookie cards. And some of those cards that she wanted to trade away eventually paid for her to go to college.

* * *

Jesus told a parable about wheat and weeds (Matt. 13:24–30, 36–43). In the parable, the farmhands want to pull up the weeds, but the farmer wisely tells them to wait. It's too early to tell the difference between wheat and weeds. If you try to pull up the weeds, you might pull up some of the wheat too. Oh, there will come a day when it's time for the harvest, and then everything gets picked—and then it will be easy to tell the difference between wheat and weeds. And the weeds will go into the fire, and the wheat will go into the barn.

The concept of harvest, with the gathering into the barn, is an allegory for the end of history, the second coming of Christ, and the gathering up of all God's people at the resurrection. There will come a time of judgment, when there will be a separation (see also Matt. 25:31–46). Some will go into the "fire" of Hell, and the others will go into the Kingdom of Heaven. But for now, in the age of the Church, we don't know who is who.

The Church Fathers liked to see this parable as a metaphor for the Church. But there were some people in the early centuries of the Church, factions who called themselves "Purists," or "Donatists," who wanted to pull the weeds. They wanted to kick all the "unrighteous" people out of the Church. But St. Augustine referred to this parable and said you don't really know who's going to Heaven and who's going to Hell. It's not for us to decide that now. We have to welcome everyone into the Church and let God sort it out later, at the time of the "harvest"—that is, at the judgment. In fact, St. Augustine said, the Church is not to be thought of as some kind of quarantine for the perfect people, keeping them safe inside while keeping the imperfect people out. Rather, the Church should be thought of as a hospital, with the clergy as her doctors, and the sacraments as her medicine. She must welcome everyone who comes, because everyone needs healing.

In the Meantime

Your cell phone will run down and stop working if you don't plug it in and recharge it regularly. In a similar way, our spirits will run down if we don't connect to our power source (God) regularly in prayer, devotion, and worship. Jesus said, "I am the vine, you are the branches. He who abides in me, and I in him, he it is that bears much fruit, for apart from me you can do nothing" (John 15:5). To "abide" is to remain. Jesus is asking us to remain "in" Him—that is, to remain connected to Him. How do we do that? The primary way we do that is through regular reception of the sacrament of the Eucharist.

Jesus also said:

> I am the bread of life; he who comes to me shall not hunger, and he who believes in me shall never thirst.... I am the living bread which came down from heaven; if anyone eats of this bread, he will live forever; and the bread which I shall give for the life of the world is my flesh.... Truly, truly, I say to you, unless you eat the flesh of the Son of man and drink his blood, you have no life in you; he who eats my flesh and drinks my blood has eternal life, and I will raise him up at the last day. For my flesh is food indeed, and my blood is drink indeed. He who eats my flesh and drinks my blood abides in me, and I in him (John 6:35, 51, 53–56).

Do you want to be raised to eternal life? Then stay connected to Jesus through the sacrament of His Body and Blood. You cannot expect to have union with God in eternity if you have no relationship with Him in this life.

Your cell phone may also be connected to "the Cloud," which (I think) is a big hard drive in the sky somewhere that stores your data, contacts, calendars, photos, and videos of your kids (or cats). A lot of people are so connected to that Cloud that, if they become disconnected, they get stressed out. I'm concerned about the way we are becoming more dependent on technology (and the services of powerful corporations). But there is another cloud—more powerful, and more important. The Letter to the Hebrews says that we are surrounded by a great "cloud of witnesses" (12:1). These are the saints, and all those who have gone before us in the Faith. Everyone waiting for you in the afterlife, from the martyrs of the early Church to your favorite uncle; they are cheering you on as you "run with perseverance the race that is set before us" (Heb. 12:1). They are praying for you. And as long as you live in this earthly life you can also remain connected to them, by praying for their intercession. They want to pray for you, and they will.

Even though the resurrection has not happened, and will not happen until the end of history, even now we are connected, by the power of the Holy Spirit, to all those in Paradise. Although the dead in Christ do not yet have their bodies back, they are worshipping God in His presence, and they are bringing our prayers before the throne of God, as it says in the book of Revelation, "the twenty-four elders fell down before the Lamb, each holding a harp, and with golden bowls full of incense, which are the prayers of the saints" (Rev. 5:8; see also 8:4). So do not miss the opportunity to ask for the intercession of your cloud of witnesses.

By the way, don't confuse this with the practice of necromancy, which is prohibited (Deut. 18:10–11). Necromancy means talking with the dead, but it refers specifically to works of the occult, such as séances, the use of Ouija boards, tarot cards, and other kinds of fortune-telling, which are ways people have tried to communicate with the dead for the purpose of gaining personal (magical) power or advantageous insights. When we pray to the saints, we are only asking for their intercession; we are not trying to access power or get them to do anything for us directly, and we do not ascribe divine powers to them (for more on this, see my book *Handed Down: The Catholic Faith of the Early Christians*). In fact, reading your horoscope is closer to the prohibited practice of necromancy than prayer to the saints is.

One last point on this topic — remember that Mary is the Queen of the Saints precisely because she is the only person in history besides Jesus who has already experienced the resurrection. The assumption of her body into Heaven *is* her resurrection, and so she lives even now with her Son in the heavenly realm — her spirit already reunited with her body. So do take advantage of the intercession of the Mother of God. Just as her intercession jump-started Jesus' ministry, she is happy to intercede with her Son on your behalf.

Eternal Life Starts Now

As Christians, we have this great hope in the resurrection. In fact, this is the hope that gives us the perspective we need to get through the hardest times in this life. But if we focus so much on our future hope of Heaven that we neglect our duties here on earth, we are failing in our mission as Christians. We need to find that balance of staying connected to Jesus and the cloud of witnesses without always having our head in the clouds. So how do we do that?

In Luke's Gospel we read of a time when Jesus was visiting the sisters Martha and Mary of Bethany (Luke 10:38–42). Martha was being the hostess and working hard at serving Jesus and His disciples. Meanwhile Mary was seated with the disciples, listening to Jesus teach. Martha complained to Jesus and asked him to tell Mary to join her in the kitchen. But it probably came as a surprise to her when Jesus told her that Mary had made a better choice. There would always be work to be done, but when it's time to be in the presence of Jesus, the work can wait. This tells us that there is a certain priority of devotion over service. As I like to say, you have to seek Christ before you can serve Him. If you don't first go to Christ and receive from Him (especially in the Eucharist), then you have nothing to give to others. So, your first priority is to "abide" in Him by going to worship and receiving the Eucharist.

Having said that, Jesus did not mean to imply that we should only worship and never work. What we receive from Christ is meant to be shared with the world by loving our neighbors. And how do we do that? Well, this is where we come full circle to the resurrection body. Remember that the resurrection body will be the same body that we inhabit now. It will be transformed and glorified, to be sure, but it will be the same body. That means that the bodies of those we see around us are God's good creation and are meant to be redeemed and raised perfected. So, our duty in this life is to care for bodies—our own, and those of the people God puts in our lives. This is what we often refer to as the corporal works of mercy.

The corporal works of mercy come in part from that passage with Jesus' teaching on the sheep and the goats in Matthew 25, where He says that whatever we do to the least of His people, we do to Him. There are slightly different versions of the list, but in general they are these:

- feeding the hungry
- giving drink to the thirsty
- clothing the naked or giving alms to the poor

• sheltering the homeless or refugees
• visiting the sick
• visiting prisoners or freeing slaves
• burying the dead

These works are not optional for Christians; they are our mission in the world. They are, in fact, the very way that the early Christians converted the Roman Empire (for more on that, see my book with Mike Aquilina *How Christianity Saved Civilization, and Must Do So Again*). Of course, we have to acknowledge that each person cannot do all of these at the same level of involvement. We are all called to different aspects of the mission, and some of us will focus on one thing, while others focus on something else. But any Christian who is not putting time into something on this list is missing an important part of the ministry to which Jesus has called all of His disciples. It could be argued that failing to engage in corporal works of mercy is a form of being "guilty of profaning the body and blood of the Lord" (1 Cor. 11:27), since every Christian's body is a member of the Body of Christ (1 Cor. 12). To fail to engage in the corporal works of mercy is to embrace that gnostic dualism that says the human body is disposable. And that is simply not what we believe. We are not spirits trapped in bodies, and we are not minds longing for freedom from the material world. We are embodied spirits — whole people made of both mind/spirit and body.

As we noted earlier, there is an aspect of the Kingdom that is present among us now. So, in a way, our eternal life has already begun, in the sense that we abide in Jesus through the sacraments of His Church, and in the sense that we participate in the work of the Kingdom through corporal works of mercy. Jesus said something that can be translated as "Behold, the kingdom of God is in the midst of you" or as "Behold, the kingdom of

God is within you" (Luke 17:21). Either way, it's true. But right now, we know God only as though we're seeing Him through a dark glass (1 Cor. 13:12). We still wait for the time when we will see Him "face-to-face." Yet, as St. Paul tells us, three things remain: our faith, which gives us peace of mind that we will be reunited with our loved ones who passed on before us; our hope, which gives us the confidence of the big picture to live through the trials of this life; and love — both the love of God for us, and our love for each other — which carries us through to the resurrection and into eternity. Faith will go away, because it will become unnecessary, when we believe by sight. Hope will go away, because it, too, will become unnecessary, when we have received what we hope for. But love will never go away, because love is eternal.

In Heaven There Ain't No Beer

I remember as a kid growing up in Milwaukee that there was a polka song that got played at every wedding. The line I remember is: "In Heaven there ain't no beer, that's why we drink it here." It doesn't sound like a very deep theological statement, but it does get at the core of the question we've been exploring: What will Heaven be like? What will *we* be like, and how will we interact with others and with the environment in which we find ourselves? And how do we prepare for Heaven now?

It turns out that "Heaven" is a kind of a catch-all term for the afterlife, but that our experience of life after death is split up into two phases. The first phase is Paradise. After we die, we go through the purification of Purgatory, and then enter Paradise. The second phase comes after the end of human history — it's the resurrection and our entry into the eternal Kingdom of God.

And in that final phase of our existence, the phase that lasts forever, there *will* be hugs in Heaven.

So, for now, take care of your body as perhaps God's greatest gift to you other than salvation. Don't abuse it, don't subject it to harsh chemicals or excessive work or stress. Do enjoy the beauty of creation and the bounty of God's provision that comes to you through the senses of your body. Seek out ways to appreciate creation in nature, art, and music. Actively thank God for good food, and yes, even beer—just don't indulge in ways that harm the body God gave you or dull your mind and lead you to make bad choices.

Also make sure to intentionally take care of the bodies of others. Reject any dualism of spirit and matter that relegates the physical body to anything less than an essential part of who we are as human beings. Give alms to the poor, volunteer at a food pantry or a homeless shelter, or volunteer at a hospital, hospice, or prison. And for the majority of us who are not called to a vocation of directly caring for the bodies of the dead, we can encourage our relatives to reject the current trend of having secularized memorial services in funeral homes or hotel banquet rooms, and insist that any Christian who dies deserves to have a funeral service in a church, preferably with a Mass, if appropriate. Finally, reject all forms of entertainment that exploit the bodies of others, even when they are willing participants. In these ways, we will honor the bodies that God created for us and that will be with us in the Kingdom.

"Ashes to ashes and dust to dust" is not the end of the story, especially if it causes us to think that the afterlife is a disembodied existence. An afterlife that is spiritual only, or mental without being physical, is not a Christian idea—it's a pagan idea. We know better. We look forward to the resurrection of the body, because even in the post-resurrection Kingdom of Heaven, we have not escaped creation. The heavenly realm is a created environment, and if we are to be part of that environment—in fact, if we are to be redeemed as whole persons and interact with other people—we will have to be there in bodies, bodies that will be raised and transformed for life in a glorified existence. Ashes will be raised and joined with ashes; and dust will be raised and joined with dust as God redeems and remakes the body for a new and eternal life.

Appendix A

The Human Being: Two Parts or Three?

Some of the Church Fathers wrote as though the human being has two parts, a body and a soul. The soul can also be called the spirit. For example, the North African Church Father Tertullian, writing around the turn of the third century, said that "a human is composed of two natures, just as Christ is" (*On the Resurrection of the Flesh* 14). Tertullian and others like him followed St. Paul in addressing the problem of original sin, which often causes our bodies and souls to pull us in different directions. The body wants to leave the game and beat the traffic. The soul wants to stick it out and see if the Packers can make that winning touchdown. The body is often impatient and shortsighted. The soul can see the bigger picture and think long-term. And that is the human dilemma.

But remember that this is not a gnostic dualism that assumes there is something inherently evil about the body. No, the body—though it is not the part of us made in the image of God—is still created by God. And anything God created is good, at least until it is corrupted by the misuse of human free will. But that's on us. The truth is that the Church Fathers did not believe in this kind of dualism because they did not believe that the body and the soul were as different, or indeed as separate, as we might assume.

What *Really* Happens after We Die

The Church Fathers did not believe (as the gnostics did) that the soul was holy and the body was evil, and they also did not believe that the soul was purely spiritual (divine) and the body purely material. The truth is, they saw both soul and body as created by a good God; so on the one hand, the soul cannot be divine or purely spiritual because only God is pure Spirit (since only God is uncreated); and on the other hand, the body is not completely different from the soul, because for the Church Fathers, everything that is created and has existence is in some way "material." This is not a dualism of spirit versus matter, because everything in the created universe is matter. It's not that the body is matter and the spirit is not, but that everything exists as degrees of matter. The soul may be made of a "lighter" or "thinner" kind of matter than the body, but it's still matter. In fact, Augustine said that even air has a material existence. (St. Augustine, *On the Soul and its Origin* 4.19. For more on this, see *Eschatology: Death and Eternal Life*, by Joseph Ratzinger [Pope Emeritus Benedict XVI] especially the section around p. 250.)

Tertullian would agree that the spirit-matter dualism is a false dichotomy. Although he used different terms to make the same points that Macrina and Augustine would make, he argues for the similarity and the very real connection of body and soul by pointing out how the senses of the body can perceive intangible things such as sound and light (*On the Resurrection of the Flesh* 17). In *A Treatise on the Soul*, Tertullian reminds his readers that when the spirit (or mind) feels embarrassed, the body blushes; when the spirit (or mind) is anxious, the body suffers; and when the body feels physical pain, the spirit suffers. What we would call the psychosomatic connection (literally, in Greek, the soul-body connection) was perceived by the Church Fathers as evidence of a very real union of the human spirit with the body. It is important to keep this in mind whenever we think about the doctrine of the resurrection of the body.

Tertullian does say, however, that there is an important difference between the spirit (or soul) and the body. While the body is composite (made up of different parts), the human spirit is *simplex*, which is to say that it is not composed of smaller parts, such as limbs, cells, molecules, and atoms. What this means is that the spirit cannot decay, because there are no smaller constituent parts into which it can decompose, and therefore it is *incorruptible*, and it can be immortal by virtue of its very nature. The human body, on the other hand, is composed of parts, so under the effects of sin, it can decay and decompose, breaking down into its smaller bits. As we have seen, if the body is to be immortal, it can be so only by virtue of the redemption that comes with resurrection.

To that end, Gregory's sister Macrina tells us that after a person's death, though the body decays, the spirit watches over all the pieces of the body and remains connected to them until they are all reunited with each other and with the spirit at the resurrection.

It may be that most people today simply think of a person as a soul (or spirit) in a body. And there is plenty of support for this idea in the Church Fathers. But it seems as though the writers of the New Testament, and perhaps most of the Church Fathers, saw the human being as having, not two, but three parts. In this way of looking at a person, the soul and the spirit are different things.

The author of the Letter to the Hebrews made this interesting comment: "For the word of God is living and active, sharper than any two-edged sword, piercing to the division of soul and spirit, of joints and marrow, and discerning the thoughts and intentions of the heart" (Heb. 4:12). The division of soul and spirit? If those are the same thing, how are they divided? Clearly, this apostolic author did not think they are the same thing. The word for "soul" here is the Greek word *psyche*, where we get our English word "psyche." So in addition to the concept of soul, it can also mean the self, or a person's life. The division of self and spirit, or life and spirit, therefore, is the separation of what we might normally call the soul (the spirit) from the life force of the body. In other words, this is physical death, when the spirit leaves the body, and the body is left with no animating force, and so it begins to decay.

Justin Martyr, the second-century Christian philosopher, wrote a document called *On the Resurrection*, in which he said: "For the body is the house of the soul, and the soul is the house of the spirit. These three, in all those who cherish a sincere hope and unquestioning faith in God, will be saved." Notice that he's very clear that the body will be saved. This is not a simple "soul goes to Heaven and leaves the body behind" view of the after-life. Justin knew that the body cannot live without the soul, but he also knew that the death of the body was not the end of the story. The ultimate end of the believer is the reunion — and the salvation — of all three: body, soul, and spirit. But also notice that he saw these three parts of the human person as something like those Russian dolls — one inside the next. The spirit is in the soul, and the soul is in the body. So, in a way, it makes sense that the human person should be made of three parts, since that seems to mirror the Trinity, but we have to keep in mind that the image of God is not all three parts, but specifically the spirit. For St. Augustine, it is in the spirit that we find the image of the Trinity, in the three subparts of memory, intellect, and will.

Other Church Fathers also believed that there was a difference between the spirit and the soul. They referred to the spirit as the "rational soul," as opposed to the "animal soul." The rational soul (the spirit) is the mind and the will, driving intentional decisions, and the animal soul is that which drives unconscious desires and bodily functions. In the ancient world, the rational soul was sometimes referred to as the heart. In the minds of the authors of Scripture, the heart was not the place of emotion, but the place where decisions were made, the seat of the will. So, when Jesus tells you to forgive people "from your heart" (Matt. 18:35), He's not saying that you have to *feel* like forgiving. He's saying you have to make a *decision* to forgive, whether you feel like it or not. We can even see this in the Old Testament. In Psalms 51:17, a Hebraic parallelism equates the broken spirit with the broken heart. The spirit *is* the heart, which for the ancients was synonymous with the mind and the will. On the other hand, the animal soul was the place where the passions come from. The seat of emotion was not your heart but your "guts."

Some Church Fathers speculated that the existence of the animal soul was not a part of the original creation of humanity but was a result of the Fall. But all those who saw spirit and soul as different things tended to talk about which one ruled the other. Of course, the Christian is supposed to do the will of God, which means making the rational soul the master over the animal soul. The spirit should rule the soul so that the soul does not lead us into temptations of the flesh.

So, what are we to say? Is the human person made of two parts or three? St. Augustine answered the question this way: "There are three things of which a person consists—namely, spirit, soul, and body; which again are spoken of as two, because frequently the soul is named along with the spirit" (*On Faith and the Creed* 10). Therefore, it seems as though it's acceptable to think of a person either way—as two parts or three—as long as we understand that whether or not there is a distinction to be made between the spirit (rational soul) and the soul (animal soul), it is not the case that one survives death and the other does not, or that one is to be redeemed and the other is not. As Justin Martyr made clear, all three (body, soul, and spirit) are to be saved.

Appendix B

We Worship with Our Bodies

Have you ever wondered why we do so much standing and kneeling in church, and why our Faith includes so much physical movement? Why don't we just sit under a palm tree and contemplate the universe, like those of other faiths? Why isn't our Faith just an intellectual exercise—a belief of the mind only? Well, by now you know that the body is an essential part of who we are, not only as human beings, but as individuals. God created us to be embodied and to interact with the rest of creation through our bodies, and so our bodies are good, and they are meant to be redeemed, not discarded. Therefore, our relationship with our Creator (not to mention the way we obey our God and love our neighbors) is one that engages our whole person, including the body and all its senses.

It's important to remember that for the first thousand years of Christianity, or more, there were no pews in churches. People stood for worship and kneeled during times of penance. Early Christians prayed in what is called the *orans* position—standing with hands raised and slightly opened—symbolically and literally opening themselves up to God (see Ps. 63:4; 134:2; 141:2; 1 Tim. 2:8). You may see people doing this today, especially during the Our Father. Some people in the early Church prayed in a cruciform position, with hands extended outward in imitation of the position Jesus endured on the Cross.

And so we pray with our whole bodies—standing, sitting, kneeling, bowing our heads, folding our hands, sometimes even prostrating ourselves (as did the Magi [Matt. 2:11] and the apostles [see Matt. 14:33; 28:9]). We face east, cross ourselves, and anoint our bodies with holy water and oil. We pray with rosary beads in our fingers, move along the Stations of the Cross, walk a labyrinth, and go on pilgrimage where we can stand on holy ground. We engage all the senses of our bodies: *seeing* statues, icons, and liturgical colors; *hearing* the words of Scripture and the music; *smelling* the incense; *touching* the holy books and the hands of our neighbors in the passing of the peace; and *tasting* the Eucharistic elements as we accept Jesus Christ into our very bodies when we receive His Body and Blood.

Christianity could never be a faith of the mind alone, because God created us to be people who are more than just a mind, but a mind with a beautiful interface with creation—our human bodies.

Other Books by James L. Papandrea

A Week in the Life of Rome

How Christianity Saved Civilization, and Must Do So Again
(with Mike Aquilina)

From Star Wars to Superman:
Christ Figures in Science Fiction and Superhero Films

The Earliest Christologies:
Five Images of Christ in the Postapostolic Age

Handed Down: The Catholic Faith of the Early Christians
(also available in Polish as *Depozyt wiary*)

ROME: A Pilgrim's Guide to the Eternal City

Trinity 101: Father, Son, Holy Spirit

Reading the Early Church Fathers

Novatian of Rome and the Culmination of Pre-Nicene Orthodoxy

The Wedding of the Lamb:
A Historical Approach to the Book of Revelation

Spiritual Blueprint: How We Live, Work, Love, Play, and Pray

The Adventures of the Space Boys:
The Space Boys Meet the Moon Bully
(with illustrations by Joe Groshek)

Sophia Institute

Sophia Institute is a nonprofit institution that seeks to nurture the spiritual, moral, and cultural life of souls and to spread the Gospel of Christ in conformity with the authentic teachings of the Roman Catholic Church.

Sophia Institute Press fulfills this mission by offering translations, reprints, and new publications that afford readers a rich source of the enduring wisdom of mankind.

Sophia Institute also operates the popular online resource CatholicExchange.com. *Catholic Exchange* provides world news from a Catholic perspective as well as daily devotionals and articles that will help readers to grow in holiness and live a life consistent with the teachings of the Church.

In 2013, Sophia Institute launched Sophia Institute for Teachers to renew and rebuild Catholic culture through service to Catholic education. With the goal of nurturing the spiritual, moral, and cultural life of souls, and an abiding respect for the role and work of teachers, we strive to provide materials and programs that are at once enlightening to the mind and ennobling to the heart; faithful and complete, as well as useful and practical.

Sophia Institute gratefully recognizes the Solidarity Association for preserving and encouraging the growth of our apostolate over the course of many years. Without their generous and timely support, this book would not be in your hands.

www.SophiaInstitute.com
www.CatholicExchange.com
www.SophiaInstituteforTeachers.org

Sophia Institute Press® is a registered trademark of Sophia Institute.
Sophia Institute is a tax-exempt institution as defined by the
Internal Revenue Code, Section 501(c)(3). Tax ID 22-2548708.